PORTRAITS FROM CANADA CAMP

Kumarian Press Books for a World that Works

GAZA

LEGACY OF OCCUPATION—
A PHOTOGRAPHER'S JOURNEY

DICK DOUGHTY
MOHAMMED EL AYDI

Kumarian Press

Kumarian Press Books for a World that Works

GAZA: Legacy of Occupation—A Photographer's Journey. Published 1995 in the United States of America by Kumarian Press, Inc., 630 Oakwood Avenue, Suite 119, West Hartford, Connecticut 06110-1529 USA.

Production supervised by Jenna Dixon
Photographs by Dick Doughty   *Maps by Deborah A. Kelly*
Copyedited by Linda Faillace   *Proofread by Beth Richards*
Text designed and typeset by Jenna Dixon
Index prepared by Mary G. Neumann

Printed in the United States of America on recycled acid-free paper by Thomson-Shore, Inc. Text printed with soy-based ink.

Library of Congress Cataloging-in-Publication Data
Doughty, Dick, 1958–
    Gaza : legacy of occupation : a photographer's journey / Dick Doughty and Mohammed El Aydi.
        p.   cm. — (Kumarian Press books for a world that works)
    Includes index.
    ISBN 1-56549-044-4
    1. Gaza Strip—Description and travel. 2. Gaza Strip—Pictorial works.
3. Refugees, Arab—Social conditions. 4. Refugees, Arab—Pictorial works.
5. Palestinian Arabs—Egypt—Social conditions. 6. Palestinian Arabs—
Egypt—Pictorial works. 7. Kanadā (Egypt : refugee camp). 8. Kanadā (Egypt : Refugee camp)—Pictorial works. 9. Doughty, Dick, 1958–   —Journeys—
Gaza Strip. 10. Doughty, Dick, 1958–   —Journeys—Egypt. I. El Aydi, Mohammed, 1963–   . II. Title. III. Series.
DS110.G3D58   1995
953'.1—dc20   94-45892

04 03 02 01 00 99 98 97 96 95   10 9 8 7 6 5 4 3 2 1   1st Printing 1995

CONTENTS

For those in Canada Camp, Egypt,
who await their homecoming still

PROLOGUE

We have bad memories of journalists. My brother met one once in Cairo. He filled a notebook just like yours. A week after that the interior police interrogated my brother and harassed him.

—Resident of Canada Camp repatriated
to the Gaza Strip

I remember it was on 15 May 1948 I left Faluja village. I was seventeen, and just married. I had a baby daughter just seven days old. My brother wanted me to leave my baby behind, just drop her, because we had to escape so fast and the Israeli planes were shooting at us. I didn't [leave the baby], but we came to Gaza with nothing. I left 400 to 500 dunums [of land]. This is why we have tried to educate ourselves, because it is all you can move with. You can't take money or land, but you always have your education. Six of my cousins died that day.

Why did you come to Gaza?
We escaped from Faluja to near Likhsas. After that, the planes came there, so we escaped to Gaza town. And when it began again in Gaza, we escaped south to Beni Suheila, near Khan Yunis. Then they attacked there. We went on south to Rafah hill. Then UNRWA [the United Nations Relief and Works Agency] began helping us survive with tents and rations. People tried to find work. And here we are.

Do you ever wish you had escaped to another country?
I was young, and it was God who saved us. In any
place now, it's the same life for us, really. For forty-
five years we've been without a country, a homeland, a solution. They deported us from our house
in Rafah Camp over to Canada Camp in Egypt and
now back to this Canada Camp [Gaza Strip] again.
Now we are just here. We need a home. This is not
really our home.

—Aziza, sixty-two, repatriated from Canada
Camp Egypt. Six of her seven children
have earned university degrees.

PREFACE

It was over an Egyptian pizza in 1989 I learned of Canada Camp. I was a month into my first job in the Middle East, as a photojournalist for *Cairo Today* magazine.

"It's the only Palestinian refugee camp in Egypt," explained my companion, a freelance reporter. "It's 5,000 people who were told they'd go back to the Gaza Strip after Camp David, but they were tricked. They're stuck on the Egyptian side of the border. Now there's an agreement to let back a few dozen families at a time over ten or twelve years. This makes them the only Palestinians ever allowed back into Israeli-occupied territory as a community. Want to shoot it?"

Even before the injustice of Canada Camp's predicament sank in, I recall asking myself, "Who, given the choice, would move *into* the Gaza Strip?" Images flew by in my mind of teeming refugee camps, sewers like open sores, shouting men masked in checkered scarves, stones flying and Israeli soldiers shooting: *intifada*—the Palestinian uprising, literally, "shaking off," against Israeli occupation then two years old—the Gaza Strip of my hometown six o'clock news. "Sure," I said, curious.

The next day, eight bus hours northeast of Cairo, we found Canada Camp pounded under July's hammer sun. Our hosts plied us with endless glasses of tea and eagerly reordered my images. Talk here was of schools, of work and the lack of it, and of wanting—passionately—to go back to the Gaza Strip. "It's not home," one man said, "but it's Palestine."

We were shown The Calling Wall, or *el silik*, "the wire," as residents say, at the edge of Canada Camp. Here, on either side of the international border, stood people. Families have met here to yell across razor wire and no-man's-land since 1982. I never forgot the faces, nor the hands, reaching.

When I returned to the U.S. six months later, I found through research that the media picture of the Gaza Strip was indeed, at the time, much as I had thought over that Cairo pizza: a sinkhole of poverty, a wellspring of irrational hatred, a netherworld where life is either unimaginable or just pathetic.

Yet now, six years later, these Gazan lives have become central to the future of the entire region. One in eight of the world's 6.5 million Palestinians live in the Gaza Strip. Under the Palestinian Authority born of the 1993 Declaration of Principles, the Gaza Strip has become a proving ground for the uncertain future of Palestine.

In 1992 I returned to Canada Camp planning to portray Gazan life as experienced by the camp's few repatriated families. Arrangements came slowly. Trust preceded efficiency at every step. I had to work exclusively among Palestinians. Under the occupation—and particularly since the *intifada*—the Gaza Strip was in *halat harb*, a condition of war. Israeli contacts of any kind were unsafe for both myself and my hosts.

Life under Israeli occupation was exhausting and traumatic. Much of what I saw and heard and felt could not be photographed, sometimes for reasons of occupation, sometimes for reasons of Gazan culture. Increasingly I relied on written notes. Within weeks, I began to sense the seeds of a different story, one that would prove more telling of daily Gazan life: a personal account of what happens along the way to doing—or trying to do—a photojournalist's job. In this book I've distilled my experiences from among both Canada Camp residents and others from January to April 1993, months that now are being remembered as a particularly hard time, but a time, too, that is crucial to understand if one is to also begin understanding the immensely complex present.

From the day we met in 1992, Mohammed El Aydi's role as host, guide, cultural consultant and, more than anything, unflagging and buoyant friend, proved so determinative at every stage of this book that he has been, all along, a coauthor. Thus this is a book inscribed not merely through cameras, film and notebooks, but through relationships.

HISTORICAL NOTE

Ten months after the signing of the September 1993 Israeli-PLO Declaration of Principles, as PLO Chairman Yasser Arafat was preparing to step from Egypt into the Gaza Strip for the first time in twenty-seven years, a small crowd of several dozen Palestinians gathered in the morning sun in front of the Egyptian border terminal. Unlike the euphoric throngs awaiting him on the Gaza Strip side, this group had more on its mind than mere well-wishing.

"Don't forget us!" they shouted. "Don't forget Canada Camp!" The Chairman glanced over, waved, and was gone into Gaza.

That the cries of 363 politically stranded families would pass unnoticed on a day of historic headlines and handshakes is perhaps to be expected. Yet Canada Camp's experience is in many ways a microcosm of the enduring predicaments faced by all Gazans today: physical confinement, political disempowerment, separations within families, dependency on foreign assistance and a halting, largely superficial "progress" framed by a daily reality residents themselves experience as appalling. Like other Gazans, Canada Camp residents today are grappling with legacies—material and emotional—of an occupation that in all too many ways has yet to end, legacies that weigh heavily upon the future, perhaps more heavily, in the end, than diplomacy.

Canada Camp, it could be said, owes its existence to Israeli General Ariel Sharon. In 1970, he commanded "Iron Fist," Israel's no-holds-barred counterinsurgency response to the Palestinian *fedayeen*, or fighters. Up and down the Gaza Strip, Iron Fist meant a month-long curfew followed by waves of beatings, imprisonments, house searches and shootings. Iron Fist also meant a new road system imposed within the eight main refugee camps. The "Sharon Streets," as the over-wide streets are wryly called even today, were plowed to permit the rapid pursuit of guerrillas into formerly labyrinthine camps. Over three years, more than 13,000 people in Gaza Strip refugee camps awoke to a black "X" on a wall outside their home. They had to choose between evacuation either to the homes of relatives elsewhere or to one of several new Israeli-designated housing projects.

One such housing project paved over an almond grove in Rafah, the old border town before Israel took control of the Sinai Peninsula in 1967. As it was built, people began calling it "Canada Camp."

"It was a joke," explained Mohammed Al Najjar, United Nations (UN) camp director until 1994. "They had just built another project to the east the people called 'Brazil' because a UN peacekeeping force from Brazil had once camped there before 1967. We said, 'Okay, if you are Brazil, then we are Canada.' We were hungry for some humor, I think. It was a terrible time, those years."

Mukhayim kanada, or Canada Camp, it was. From 1973 to 1975, 496 extended families—just under 5,000 people— moved in.

Residents now say they knew perfectly well Canada Camp lay on the old Egyptian side of the border. In the mid-1970s, however, nobody thought this mattered because the border had been history since 1967. Canada Camp was one of several neighborhoods within Rafah, population then approaching 60,000. Canada Camp men and women worked up and down the Gaza Strip, and men toiled among the 75,000 day workers in Israel. Canada Camp children attended school in Rafah. All Canada Camp shopped in Rafah's tattered and sprawling markets.

The troubles for Canada Camp began in 1982. It was April 25, the day the Camp David Accords bore their final fruit. On that day, Israel completed its handover to Egypt of the occupied—and settled—Sinai Peninsula. In return, Egypt made official its peace with Israel. In Rafah, the Egypt-Israel border would revert to its pre-1967 line.

There was, however, a problem: Canada Camp lay on the Egyptian side. The fence would have to dogleg around three

At the Calling Wall, Canada Camp, Egypt, a woman keeps her weekly appointment to speak with her sister on the Gaza Strip side. (Made with the permission of the woman photographed in the presence of an Egyptian government press guide.)

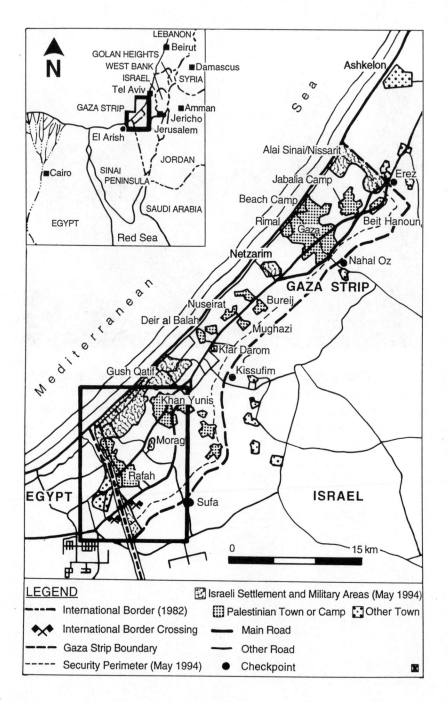

LEGEND

- – · – · – International Border (1982)
- ◆◆ International Border Crossing
- – – – Gaza Strip Boundary
- – – – Security Perimeter (May 1994)

- Israeli Settlement and Military Areas (May 1994)
- Palestinian Town or Camp
- Other Town
- Main Road
- Other Road
- ● Checkpoint

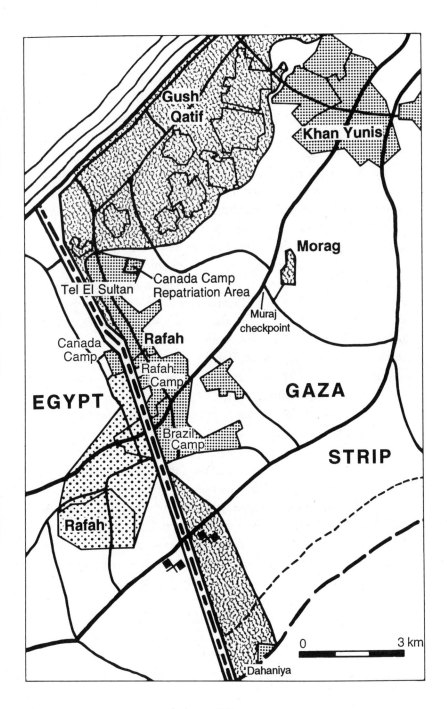

Gush
Qatif ×

Khan Yunis

Morag

Canada Camp
Repatriation Area

Tel El Sultan

Muraj
checkpoint

Canada
Camp

Rafah

Rafah
Camp

GAZA

Brazil
Camp

EGYPT

STRIP

Rafah

0   3 km

Dahaniya

sides of the camp to include it in the Gaza Strip. But neither Egypt nor Israel would countenance disturbance of the otherwise straight, historically logical line.

Two days before the border was finalized, Israeli and Egyptian authorities announced their resolution of Canada Camp's problem to six members of Canada Camp's leadership. Israel promised relocation for families in Tel el Sultan, another housing project two miles north. Egyptian officials promised an unspecified compensation for homes left behind in Canada Camp. "We were assured it would all happen within six months," said Najjar, "according to the terms written in Camp David." Until relocation, camp residents would receive permits for unfettered passage across the new border.

The next day, Egyptian and Israeli soldiers unrolled coil upon coil of razor wire and sliced Rafah in half, Berlin-style. As mandated in the Camp David accords, the southern part of the town reverted to Egypt, and the northern part remained under Israeli occupation, becoming what is today the southern terminous of the Gaza Strip. For the 4,500 residents of Canada Camp, this day is remembered as *youm iswid*, "a black day," the day the long waiting began.

Instead of issuing crossing permits, Israeli officials swept through Canada Camp unscrewing car license plates and cutting notches into identification documents. Soldiers who arrived to stand duty at the three border gates allowed passage, however, for a couple of days as talk of permits continued.

But then the talks stopped. No permits would be issued. As soldiers began refusing passage between Canada Camp and Rafah proper, panic and disbelief overwhelmed the camp. Children ran to alert relatives to come home—or go home—depending on which side they were on. Many people who pleaded were let through one last time, but not all. Some didn't get the news in time. They faced life apart from their parents, from their children, from their relatives. The door had been slammed and locked. Between Canada Camp and the Gaza Strip now lay *el silik*, the wire, thirty yards of no-man's-land, The Calling Wall.

Canada Camp, Egypt. Seven of every ten adult men lack full-time work. The graffiti reads, "filisteen hara," "Free Palestine."

Work permits were approved a few months later for fewer than fifty of the hundreds of men who demanded return to their jobs. Canada Camp's school had to go to three daily shifts. Egypt stamped each resident's document with a six-month visa that forbade work. Separated families were ignored. So were the promises of speedy repatriation.

Today, Israel has no self-interest in unlocking its gates any faster than it is forced to by overpopulated Egypt, which has no self-interest in assimilating Canada Camp. To this day, the residents are forbidden to work or own property outside the camp, and survive only by an infuriating dependency on a relief arm of the United Nations, the United Nations Relief and Works Agency (UNRWA). Of all sixty-one Palestinian refugee camps in the Middle East, Canada Camp has become the poorest of them all.

Economically, UNRWA classifies 75 percent of Canada Camp as "hardship cases" eligible for bimonthly staple rations. In contrast, in other Gaza Strip camps, until mid-1993 only

10 percent qualified for such relief. Visits by Canada Camp families back into the Strip are permitted for up to three months in a year; however, adult visas come with a price tag of the equivalent of US$150 per month per person, and permission is not, residents say, always granted upon request.

In enduring the separation of families, Canada Camp residents make up a small part of a regional humanitarian problem. The Palestinian human rights agency Al Haq estimates that throughout the West Bank and Gaza Strip, one in every five families—or a total of 80,000 Palestinian families—suffers an involuntary separation among immediate family members. Vastly more suffer separation among extended family members.

But in Canada Camp a unique, more violent kind of family separation has arisen. Since 1984, Egyptian authorities have deported an estimated 70 to 100 men under secret charges of political activity. Sources outside the camp say most deportees now live among Palestinian military forces in Libya, but others reside in Yemen, Sudan and Algeria. "These are the secret exiles," wrote a Palestinian lawyer, one of few to investigate the situation. Nearly all were tortured in detention prior to their deportation.[1]

In 1986 Egypt and Israel signed a slow, cumbersome framework permitting thirty-five Canada Camp families to come home each year to the Gaza Strip. Israel gridded out 200 square meters of land—about ¹⁄₂₀ of an acre—for each family in the sands of Tel el Sultan. Israel then required each to receive $12,000 cash construction assistance before the family could be granted a land title. This assistance would come from the PLO.

The instability brought on by the 1987 *intifada* delayed the first families' crossing until December 1989. By August 1992, three annual repatriation cycles had passed, and 105 of Canada Camp's nearly 500 families had moved. But PLO support of Iraq in the 1991 Gulf War had provoked Gulf Arab governments to cut off the PLO's bankroll. Canada Camp's $12,000 assistance checks fell victim to the resulting financial crisis. The door closed again.

In October 1993, following the September signing of the Declaration of Principles, the government of Canada announced it would revive the repatriation account with humanitarian aid. By July 1994, the first of the seventy families scheduled to repatriate in the 1993 and 1994 cycles received checks for $12,000 and, with the funds, registered for land titles in Tel el Sultan, Gaza Strip. However, as this book went to press, the remaining 293 families—about 3,500 people—still have no repatriation schedule. In April 1995, they entered the fourteenth year of waiting in Canada Camp.

Note

1. To date, international human rights monitoring organizations have passed over Canada Camp concerning this matter. Organizations active in Egypt, such as Middle East Watch and the Egyptian Organization for Human Rights, find Canada Camp remote, and its problems less pressing than harsh treatments meted out in more accessible, urban areas. Furthermore, residents of Canada Camp are entirely unwilling to broach the subject of human rights inside Egypt, for the camp is closely—some say intensely—monitored by informers of Egypt's State Security Investigation, the domestic security forces commonly known as *mukhabarat*, or "intelligence." Palestinian human rights organizations in the Occupied Territories such as Al Haq and the Gaza Center for Rights and Law generally consider Canada Camp outside the scope of their mandates. Amnesty International considers Canada Camp deportees outside its scope because most are deported under charges of membership in militant factions or arms smuggling that disqualify them—despite the fact these charges go uncontested in any court—as "prisoners of conscience." For this book, testimony concerning human rights abuses of Canada Camp residents was gathered both outside Egypt and the Gaza Strip from more than a half dozen sources who insisted on complete anonymity. The most common methods of torture, sources agreed, include hanging by hands tied behind the back and prolonged beatings while blindfolded. This accords with the 1992 findings of Middle East Watch that "a pattern of abuse" pervades the Egyptian prison system, despite official pronouncements to the contrary. In 1989, Canada Camp resident Abdel Baset Khalifa, age twenty-five, died during ten days of State Security Investigation interrogation; his body was found in his Rafah workshop, an act residents interpreted as an attempt by Egyptian authorities to make his death look accidental. In 1994, an estimated half dozen Canada Camp deportees living in Libya were allowed to reenter the Gaza Strip under the employ of the Palestinian National Authority; it is unclear, at the time this book went to press, how many more will be permitted to return in the future.

From a rooftop, Tel el Sultan. What are the relationships among those who write and those who are written about?

CHAPTER 1

THE NIGHT SEARCH

For three hours Mohammed and I have sat in Rowhi's windowless living room. Peeling-paint walls of flat concrete make me imagine we are actually at the bottom of a tiny, out-of-season swimming pool. Three of Rowhi's kids show off for the visitors, and their yelps echo off unforgiving walls. From under a blanket on a worn couch slip tumbling curls of hair from a small girl's head. She whimpers disconsolately from time to time. Frying oil hisses from the kitchen, a faint sweetness against Mohammed's cigarette smoke.

I hunch next to him. The house is unheated in the damp Gazan winter. His gray tweed jacket droops loosely over his thin shoulders. A Sears & Roebuck lambs-wool sweater, a present from my arrival four days ago, warms him between the jacket and a pressed, button-down shirt. Rowhi wears tweed, too, a greenish blend with leather elbow patches. The creases in his pants are sharp. United Nations professionals, both of them. I keep my black denim jacket buttoned against the chill and heat my hands on the small glass of syrupy tea.

Mohammed smokes as enthusiastically as he talks. He is balding and in his early thirties, which makes me a bit his elder, but experience has treated my features lightly by comparison. Everybody here pegs me for twenty-two or twenty-three. Indeed I feel like a much younger, entirely naive cousin here, the newcomer to whom every detail of what Gazans have come to think of as normal must be explained patiently.

I accept a cigarette when Mohammed offers one, even though I don't smoke and can't do this more than once a day without getting nauseated. His smile through his beard when he holds the cigarette out to me is boyish and irresistibly mischievous. From the moment we met last summer, this became

1

a little social ritual between us. But I also accept it because I'm becoming deeply agitated. As he and Rowhi converse in rapid Arabic that I can only dimly understand, and as we await a lunch promised hours ago, I scratch silent complaints into my yellow notebook. Our afternoon is slithering away, our opening day of our documentary of Canada Camp ground under this millstone of social ritual. As I write, I know I'm wrong in this feeling, but I can't exorcise it: all the families who have come to the Gaza Strip from Canada Camp Egypt live just a few blocks away from where we sit. I've worked toward this beginning on and off for four years and now, so close . . . but something deeper than lunch, something darker and far more Gazan, holds us fast.

Rowhi supervises Mohammed and eight other social workers at the United Nations Social Welfare Office in Rafah town. They are also good friends. I see this in the way they sit just inches from each other and touch each other frequently as they talk. This morning, however, Rowhi didn't show up at work. Mohammed and the others are worried. There is no telephone in the Rafah Social Welfare Office.

"We can go to his house," Mohammed told me when I arrived, employing his gracious way of saying we really must go. "It is not like him to do this. God knows what might have happened." Mohammed is sparing when it comes to contractions in English.

The rented, ground-floor apartment Rowhi calls his house is, only coincidentally, on the far side of Tel el Sultan, almost next door to the Canada Camp repatriates' sector.

He answered our knock wearing flannel pajamas, his squinting eyes recessed like cliff dwellings under the wall of his heavy brow. It was just past noon.

"Thank God you are here! Are you sick, or what?" asked Mohammed, hiding no euphoria to see him safe and at home.

"No, I was just sleeping. Come in, please, welcome, welcome, I'm fine now," Rowhi said, mixing English with his Arabic. "Just a terrible night. We had soldiers."

After he dressed and we removed our shoes, his wife, whose

thick hand I shook in brief introduction, delivered a tray with a metal teapot and three glasses, and disappeared.

"It was about 10 o'clock, I think, it seemed like about fifty of them out there," said Rowhi. "But I don't know exactly, I couldn't see and we were sleeping. Six of them pounded on the door"—he made a motion of using a rifle butt for this—"so I had to let them in."

"What happened?" I prompted him in English, the second language of every Palestinian UN professional.

"They lined up, inside here. One shouted he wanted to see everyone out in the hall, by the door. I brought the children out, and my wife, and we all just stood there while they looked in all the rooms. The girls started crying, and I was waiting for them to start beating us at any moment. You cannot imagine this feeling. I can say nothing. Then they asked if one man was in the house. 'No,' I said, 'He is not my family.' 'So do you know him,' they asked. I said, 'Okay, yes, he is my landlord.' They asked where he lives. 'Upstairs,' I had to tell them."

He shrugged and slumped a bit as if to make clear his distaste for such cooperation under duress.

"What would have happened if you hadn't?" I asked.

Rowhi's tone said his reply was common knowledge. "If the man is a wanted one, then they suspect me, too. They would beat me, or even the children, smash things in the house, take me to prison, you never know! That is the problem. They do anything they want."

But they didn't hit anyone. They left, and in a few minutes kicked and rifle-butted Rowhi's landlord, blindfolded and handcuffed, into a jeep and disappeared, as they always do. Relatives have been talking to a lawyer this morning to find out the charges.

"But that was not all," he continued. "Rula, she is two, you see her now"—he pointed to the teary bundle of brown curls on the couch—"she caught a fever last night of more than 103 degrees. It was so sudden, maybe one hour later."

Rowhi says he slipped out to the house of a friend who has one of Tel el Sultan's eighteen residential telephone lines. His walk was a calculated risk: military curfew keeps all 850,000 Gazans deadbolted indoors from 7:00 P.M. to 4:00 A.M., hours during which only the Israeli army and occasional Jewish settlers prowl the Gazan streets. As a UN supervisor, however, Rowhi bore in his hand his coveted red curfew pass. From his friend's house, he called one of the two ambulances that serve the more than 200,000 people of the southern Gaza Strip.

Five miles north, in Nasser Hospital, Rula's fever broke in a few hours.

"The doctor said it was not a virus. He said he had seen children before like this, very young ones, develop fevers just after being frightened, usually after the army comes into the home at night. He said take her home, let her sleep, give her lots of attention, play with her."

For Rula that night, I realized, one of the most universal of childhood fears had come to pass: monsters in the night. Not just one, but six of them right at the door, then in the house, boots and helmets and guns and walkie-talkie voices in front of which she could see her parents were powerless. In the Gaza Strip, where hundreds have been killed, thousands have been imprisoned and tens of thousands have been injured, such a nighttime raid never, ever makes the news. It is part of the life that has come to be thought of as ordinary here. The number of such raids is far beyond counting.

A survey by the Gaza Community Mental Health Program showed that for nine out of ten Gazans born since 1967, monsters in the night is the first and most frequent experience of occupation. It is nearly always a Gazan child's first meeting with a citizen of Israel. Some children, particularly those in the poorest camps, experience it dozens of times over the years. Fully half the children in the Strip have watched the soldier/monsters attack and beat parents and older siblings in the home. Only a few less have been attacked inside the home themselves.

Not Rula, though, not last night.

Recalling Rowhi's story makes me sheepish about missing our first day with the Canada Camp families. Our visit is therapy. We talk about middle-class professional stuff: their office, my toddling Arabic and what Mohammed and I plan to do for the Canada Camp story when we get around to it. For grown-ups, too, tea, cigarettes and company can chase nightmares away. Rowhi is more important than our day's work: This, I will learn, is axiomatic to Gazan life. And what Gazans call *el wadd'a*, or "the situation"—meaning the occupation and the complex array of necessary social responses—is in control. Not us.

A small feast of chicken, saffron rice, salad, cake, oranges and hot, fresh bread appears on trays and in bowls, the gift of Rowhi's wife's past three hours of solitary kitchen toil. Rula gets up at her father's beckoning, rubs her eyes, nibbles a few bites, and withdraws to play with the nearest toy: a soldier.

CHAPTER 2
SULTAN'S HILL

After lunch, with less than an hour left to the working day, Mohammed, Rowhi and I amble over the littered sand from his house to the camp. Everyone calls this Canada Camp, too, even though the original Canada Camp is back on the Egyptian side of the border, and to me this doesn't even look like a camp at all. It's more like a middle-class neighborhood, Gaza style. But say "*mukhayim kanada*" to any Rafah taxi driver and this is where he'll take you. I've taken to saying "Canada Camp Egypt" or "Canada Camp Palestine" when context doesn't keep the two places distinct. This is Canada Camp Palestine. At least we have time for a brief visit to Hanan.

As we approach, I'm struck again by how small the camp really is. Several dozen two- to five-story houses squat before us like a child's blocks set out in a sandbox. One paved road circles their perimeter. Some are painted white or pastel tones; others bare gray concrete to the wind. Reinforcing steel bars spring from flat roofs in sharp cowlicks. Some windows have glass or bars; others yawn emptily. There is an interrupted look to the place, as if well-meant plans have come to pass only by half.

North of us lie treeless, undulating low dunes, speckled with decaying carcasses of white Peugeot 404 sedans, the most common automobile in the Strip. To the west, silhouettes of distant prefab houses, trailers and towers, Israeli settlements, scratch at the horizon. Behind us sprawls the rough tapestry of gray, flat-roofed houses, the mass of the Tel el Sultan government housing project. The name translates "Sultan's Hill," but it looks no more like a hill than Canada Camp looks like a camp. It's a sandy plateau rising ever-so-gently 50 to 100 feet above a shallow depression between it and Rafah town. It was one of six communities set up by the Israeli government in the mid- to late 1970s, ostensibly to ease crowding in the refugee camps that had more than doubled their populations since 1948. This "development," however, moved less than 10 percent of the Strip's refugee camp population. It was at least as much counterinsurgency as it was humanitarianism, based on the logic that people from permanent houses have less incentive to become guerrillas than people from refugee houses. Of the government housing areas, Tel el Sultan was the largest. Most of its original population moved locally, from Rafah and Shaboura Camps, the second-largest refugee camp complex in the Gaza Strip.

Now, 10,000 people live in Tel el Sultan. It has become a kind of a suburb of Rafah, although it offers none of the quietude and relative security that comes with the Chicago suburbs I grew up in. The quarter-mile by half-mile sector of Tel el Sultan allocated to Canada Camp repatriates was surveyed into more than 600 family plots of about forty by sixty feet, or just over 200 yards square. Because families repatriated since 1989 number only 105, or one-fifth of Canada Camp Egypt, their houses pack only the northwest end of the area. Power lines crisscross the remaining, garbage-strewn expanse where impromptu soccer fields have scraps of steel reinforcing bar for goalposts.

Among the houses of Canada Camp Palestine there is still more sand. It's the powdery kind that climbs halfway to the ankles, making walking an effort. Hanan, whose house we approach, is principal of Rafah Elementary Girls School "D." She and Mohammed are distant cousins through a marriage in their parents' generation.

I recognize the freshly painted, white stucco house, two floors, with the blue trim. Last summer, Mohammed brought me here on one of my several early day-trips from Jerusalem. Hanan is one of the camp's well-known residents, and one of only a handful of female professionals. She opens the metal door, adjusting her paisley head scarf. Her eyes open wide in surprise, two brown lamps deep below lids made heavy by the blackening kohl. We shake hands, lightly and very briefly; she motions us to a brown velour couch. Her husband is not home from work yet, but because Mohammed is a relative, it is socially acceptable for us men to visit her anyway. I hand Hanan an envelope of photographs from my afternoon at her house last summer. There had been no point mailing it: that can take months, and all mail into the Gaza Strip is subject to Israeli censorship.

The living room is white and flawless. We sit beneath a twinkling chandelier in which all the lights work, our shoeless feet on an Egyptian carpet. The glass cabinets across the room are dusted. Not like my idea of a refugee camp at all. She has done well with the United Nations. In a few minutes she brings tea in cups with handles, served on saucers, and asks me to remind her if I have children.

"No," I say politely, "but, *insha'allah* . . ." I let my voice fade and hope my invocation of God's will is appropriate.

"Why not?" she parries bluntly. Her English is slow, like a truck in low gear. "You are married, aren't you? How long now?" Her hands rest on her hips, the lines in her face set.

I smile, and Mohammed laughs without inhibition. Hanan looks puzzled at what seems to be inside humor. I defer to Mohammed to explain in Arabic.

"We're laughing," he says, holding his hands out, "because last summer Dick told me everyone in Gaza always asks him exactly the same four questions when they meet him, and always in the same order. First, 'Where are you from?' Then, 'Are you married?' Third, 'Do you have children?' And number four, because he always says no to the third, 'Why not?!'"

Rowhi and Hanan take this with good humor, but Hanan's round, lined face quickly shifts from amusement to a kind of skeptical, maternal admiration. "It is important, yes, okay, you know this about us very well," she says. "And I myself have six girls. All so beautiful. And they are educated, each of them. Do you have a picture of your wife? Her name was—what was it—Kathy?"

I am touched by her memory. "Yes," I say.

"I would like to have a picture of her, to keep."

"I think I can find one." I promise to bring it next time.

Conversation turns to Rowhi's experience last night. By the time he has finished his tale, we must go. I want to ask Hanan about arranging accommodation with a family in the camp— not, of course, at her house with six unmarried daughters— but Mohammed insists there isn't time left. Curfew is in two hours at seven; the shared "service" taxis, the only type of transportation available, run only until 6:15, an arrangement that allows the drivers to get home in time. From here to Mohammed's house in Khan Yunis can take an hour.

In the taxi, I ask Mohammed what the soldiers who came to Rowhi's might have done if they had found an American photographer living with the family.

"Maybe nothing. Maybe it would help them at the time. But later," he says, pausing, sounding tired, "when you have left, maybe then they would make some problems."

I'm too tired myself to get specific, but I get the idea.

The Social Welfare Office of Rafah UNRWA—a merciful acronym for United Nations Relief and Works Agency for Palestine Refugees in the Near East—must be entered through a hole. Past a row of single-story houses of Shaboura Camp, down a dirt alley puddled with sewage, a jagged gap interrupts a concrete wall. Inside, the office occupies two worn classrooms in a former youth club compound whose gates were welded shut in 1988, the first year of the *intifada*. Then, Mohammed tells me, kids would stand on the seven-foot walls of the compound and stone Israeli army jeeps passing on the main road. The tear gas and shootings that followed didn't fit the UN's definition of recreation, so the club was closed. Now, five years later, the glassless windows are shuttered and every wall is a mural of bold, hasty graffiti.

It is Sunday and, as in much of the Muslim world, today begins the working week. The office is full of mostly elderly men and women who mill and cluster noisily around seven wooden desks. Dog-eared notebooks and boxes of index cards are tumbled about wooden tables and shelves. Everything seems dusty. Nothing is new. It's been particularly busy here, Mohammed told me earlier, since the Gulf War. With the war, both West Bank and Gaza Strip Palestinians lost nearly all the remitted wages of relatives working in the Gulf that made up nearly one-third of total family income. So far, this winter has been bad, too: fourteen days of round-the-clock military curfew in December caused a UN-estimated $28 million in lost wages and rotted winter crops. Unemployment hovers steady around 40 percent. The Social Welfare Office determines a family's eligibility for emergency rations of flour, oil, sugar, milk and other staples.

Mohammed isn't at his desk. I shake hands with Rowhi, a gentle ritual that endures into the beginning of our conversation. These prolonged handshakes feel more like an expression of heartfelt greeting than the firm, aggressive assertions with which I am familiar in the West. "Mohammed will meet you this afternoon," he says, still holding my hand, "and until then you can go back to Canada with another friend of ours." He introduces Mustafa El Hawi, civil engineer, resident of Canada Camp Palestine and good speaker of English, and excuses himself back to the crowd around his desk.

Mustafa is a taut, energetic man, mid-thirties, clean-shaven and dressed in a brown, faux-leather, vinyl jacket. His wide eyes don't blink much, and his brow carries that pent-up tension that is growing familiar. He informs me at once that he studied engineering for six months in Houston, Texas, and that he liked the United States very much. He's helped most of the Canada Camp returnees build their Tel el Sultan houses. But now, he adds, in his lightly accented English, with no families coming since last August, he works in construction as a day laborer in Israel. I sense he wants to talk; I pull out my notebook and ask how life has changed since he came back from Canada Camp Egypt.

"I'm just running now. I'm just spending all my time running to get this fucking permit," he says, showing off his English a bit and unfolding for me a blue paper covered in computer-printed Hebrew. It allows him, he explains, to join the 30,000-strong workforce of day laborers for four months.

"I remember Houston. It was so beautiful there. You know the chicken Kentucky Fried?"

I nod.

"But you know, one time I went over to my neighbor's house to meet them. They were good people, and we talked, but then I never saw them again. Never! Here we have warmer relations among neighbors, where we visit and ask about each other's health and so on every couple days or weeks. This is just our custom. But now all I do is run back and forth to Israel to cover my basic expenses, and still it's never enough. I have four children. That's all I'm thinking about. Where—how—what do I do—it is too difficult. There isn't time for good relations anymore. Not like we had in Canada Camp Egypt."

"So it is harder than you expected?" I prompt.

"You know, we were thinking in Canada Camp Egypt that most of the people here [in the Gaza Strip] were saving much more money than we were. And we wanted to be living as soon as possible here with our relatives. But now it is the inverse feeling, totally. Really it is."

"So things were better on the Egyptian side?" I say, writing notes as I speak. "Everyone there still tells me they want to come back here."

"It changed with the Gulf War. Getting work became impossible here. Then there was inflation. And the army starts bothering and frightening our children, who are not familiar with the situation here. The children get scared by the masked men, too, who come into the camp and write graffiti. We feel like we are strangers in this situation."

He accompanies me to Hanan's house for our scheduled visit, where we wait for Mohammed. I hand Hanan the photograph of my wife she asked for last time. She smiles more broadly than I have seen and compliments Kathy as "too beautiful." After my conversation with Mustafa, I want Hanan's opinion, too, of life in the Strip following her move from Canada Camp.

"I have become so sad here," she begins slowly, her elbows resting on her knees. "The life is too expensive. In the beginning, we were very happy, very enthusiastic." A look of disgust or regret or self-pity passes over her. "But now everything is too dear. And we live too far from everything. I am not young and walking in this sand is too difficult. Do you have any more pictures of your family?"

The request takes me aback and forces me out of my interviewer role. Perhaps I was too hasty in adopting it. I had barely finished my tea. I pull out a packet of photographs I keep in the top of my camera bag: our apartment in Missouri; my parents; our friends, and so on.

Hanan's husband, Abu Rashid, arrives as we look at the photos. He's a tall man with an easy, slightly comical smile and a paunch that bulges the middle of his gray, shoulder-to-floor gown, his *jalabeeya*. Sort of a stretched-out Buddha, I think. He dangles prayer beads from one hand.

Hanan carries in a photo album from another room. Here, she points, is her and Abu Rashid's wedding in 1971, a few months before the Israeli army bulldozed their house for a "Sharon Street" in Rafah refugee camp, prompting their move to Canada Camp Egypt. Here is a group portrait of the teachers at the Canada Camp Egypt school taken before the family returned to Tel el Sultan. Here is the family next to a camel at the Great Pyramid outside Cairo six or seven or maybe eight years ago. "We could go to all these places when we lived in Canada Egypt," Hanan says. "We could go to the beach, too. And now? We only stay here, in Tel el Sultan. The beach is controlled by Israel and it is too difficult to leave Gaza Strip."

I ask all three about my wish to live in Tel el Sultan. This turns the conversation awkward. Nothing is said directly. After many clarifying questions, I gather that because the families are newcomers, many would fear that other, more senior residents would think that a family hosting a U.S. journalist was in fact collaborating with Israel by hosting an undercover spy. The journalist-spy could pass the names of activists to the authorities. I also gather that because most houses are occupied by extended families, there just may not be space anywhere.

My accommodations at the western edge of Gaza city are in the meantime embarrassingly lavish. Rimal is the lone elite district of the city. For millennia, until shortly after World War I, it was a crowded port, a shipping point along trade roads stretching from Arabia to Europe, and from Asia to Africa. Now, many of Gaza's prominent doctors, businessmen, academics and land-owners live here. Many hold family names traceable for centuries. Several dozen expatriate foreign aid workers also cluster here, renting spacious flats and whole villas at fire-sale prices from families who have emigrated to the United States, Europe and the Arabian Gulf. At the beginning of the *intifada*, Mohammed told me, camp dwellers joked that the children of Rimal pelted Israeli soldiers with the chocolate bonbons they find more abundant in Rimal than stones. Rimal is the only part of the Strip where I can walk without fear of harassment either from a passing army jeep or from boys who might decide I am Israeli and thus deserving of stoning. Still, not all Rimal's streets are paved. Villa walls are covered with graffiti as often as not. In vacant lots, goats munch rotting garbage.

Here, in a cavernous, third-floor apartment where footsteps reverberate in booming echoes off a cold stone floor, I have a room to myself. It feels like a cloister, a spare hideaway from the pressing urgency of the rest of the Strip. My American hosts, an English teacher and a UN-sponsored human rights monitor, have made it that way on purpose. Refuge is essential under stress. From my room, I look out through the window's veil of palm branches across the road into Ansar II, one of two main Israeli prisons in the Strip, home to 900 Palestinian men, nearly all of whom (according to testimonies received by the Gaza Center for Rights and Law and other international human rights agencies) have been tortured. To the left lies a vacant lot half carpeted in garbage. To the right, just a few hundred yards off, a bold, oblivious intrusion of beauty sparkles and softens and on clear evenings flashes gold: the Mediterranean. Except for the occasional bark of a prison megaphone, the place is silent. It can be eerie.

I've made arrangements to process my film in a private black and white lab in Israeli-annexed, Palestinian East Jerusalem. No one has such facilities in the Strip, where only tiny, family-snapshot color labs and portrait studios dot the towns and camps. Use of a lab in Israel, Mohammed and others warned me, would bring suspicion about who would look at my film. From the apartment I pack three bags to visit East Jerusalem overnight—film to process, cameras in case anything happens along the way, and clothes. As I leave, the winter sun is lighting another cloudless sky, even though this is normally the rainy season.

From Rimal to the Jerusalem taxi station in Gaza city is about three miles inland. I hail a decrepit, white Peugeot 404 sedan, a one-shekel (forty-cent) shared taxi.

"The town?" I check in Arabic before getting in.

"Yes, get in."

"Peace be upon you," I say, pronouncing the formal greeting quickly and nonchalantly to the driver and the two men in the back. Most people in Gaza taxis are men, but not exclusively.

"And on you peace," one responds just as casually.

After I have settled my camera bag under the seat, the driver asks, "Where are you from?"

"America." This is easier than "United States" in Arabic.

"Journalist?"

"Yes. Photojournalist."

"Ah," the driver says, "photojournalist. What do you think of our situation?"

I don't feel like talking much. "You know, there are many problems, many problems," I say, pausing. "But today, there is sunshine in winter, thanks to God. Where are you from?"

"Shaja'eyya."

This is a part of Gaza city, but I'm not sure where. I just nod, say, "Uh-huh," and look out the window. Such conversations establish a rapport I, as a foreigner, depend upon for safety. My vague response to "what do you think of our situation?" communicated sympathy with the Palestinian predicament without indicating a desire to discuss details, as if the question was by now boring. It's not—I just wasn't in the mood. Mentioning the sunshine turned us to a pleasant thought and credited it to God, which is a common manner of speaking throughout the Arab world. By asking where the driver was from, I reciprocated his interest in me, establishing a measure of mutual respect. I then felt safe he wouldn't suspect me as hostile, and he seemed assured I was a real photojournalist and not an undercover spy. Downtown, he graciously points me to the Jerusalem taxis. I thank him, handing him my shekel fare.

Morning in Palestine Square, downtown Gaza city, is either a festival or a riot, depending on which side of bed you got up on. Two narrow, main streets collide and explode into a bus station, a taxi station, a fruit market, a hospital and dozens of shops and vendors. There are no traffic signals. Taxi drivers wave both hands and shout destinations as if hailing distant ships; women with baskets on their heads negotiate paths through the gridlocked mass of bleating cars and occasional horse carts. Through it all, boys drift and dart like blowing bits of paper.

Around the square, there is no building freshly painted nor clean, nor whose lower walls are not layered in graffiti, *sahafit is-shaab*, "popular journalism," the Strip's only indigenous mass media under occupation. The disarray and decay is the poverty of wartime. Although it is not the worst-looking place the world offers, it is a struggle for me, raised in the Judeo-Christian tradition, not to look upon Palestine Square and see here ground zero of the living antithesis of the myth of The Promised Land.

The Jerusalem taxis are seven-passenger, stretch Mercedes cars. I'm a fourth passenger, so I write as we await three more. That can take awhile these days: since the Gulf War, Israel requires permits for Palestinians aged sixteen to sixty traveling from one section of the occupied West Bank and Gaza Strip to another. This, in a subtle way, has unofficially cantonized the territories. Mohammed, although his record is "clean," hasn't left the Strip in two years. Too complicated, he says; too many questions, too much time lost waiting at offices.

Palestine Square hasn't always marked the center of the city. From the obscure days when Gaza was founded, probably about 4,000 years ago by early frankincense traders from what is now Yemen, the central square stood about a half mile east, where the main mosque stands today. Palestine Square lies at the edge of the old city, once walled and overlooking vegetable and barley farms, olive and almond groves. "Like a cloth of brocade spread out upon the land," wrote Syrian scholar al-Dimashki in the late 1300s. But the city walls have been gone exactly 801 years now, felled by the Crusader army of Richard the Lion-Hearted under his disarmament treaty with Saladin, liberator of Jerusalem and one of the most revered figures in Arab history. At the same time, Richard tore down the castle that stood in Gaza, but no one has ever found a trace of it. He left, however, the giant church the Crusaders built during their time in the city and today, with minor modifications added in the fourteenth century, it serves as the central mosque, the Mosque of Omar.

In those bygone eras it was trade that made Gaza rich, and geography made it one of the most contested cities in the world. By 1500 B.C., Gaza's name meant "the ruler's prize" to ancient Egyptians, who quickly realized the city was a door between Egypt and Syria, even between all of Africa and Asia. Other powers noted this no less astutely: the city has known occupation by Egyptians, Persians, Babylonians, Greeks, Seleucids, Syrians, Assyrians, Judeans, Israelites, seven centuries of Romans, Seljuk Turks, Muslim Arabs, Crusaders, Egyptian Mamluks, Ottoman Turks, the French, the British, the Egyptians again, and now Israel.

A passing army jeep plugs in the present again. The soldier riding in the back leans over his M-16 that he keeps propped on his knee, casually eyeballing the gunsight at the windows in our line of taxis. I stare, but nobody else seems to. My eyes meet his for an instant over the barrel, and he's gone.

The taxi fills within half an hour. We ride in silence through Israel's fields, stoplights and gas stations to the stony sidewalks and graffiti-covered shop doors of East Jerusalem.

In a tiny darkroom under a flight of stairs, I scan two rolls from my days with Mohammed in Tel el Sultan. I think about what I am choosing to photograph, and the relationships that are evolving from our activity. What am I taking, giving, doing? I make a few prints to bring to Mohammed, Mustafa, Rowhi and Hanan—the least I can do. I'm obsessed right now with "ordinariness." Rank, plain, dumb, simple daily life; kids and food and work and resisting the occupation. Why?

I think it's my reaction to legions of other photographs from "hot spots" around the world—Gaza is certainly one—that show them as relentlessly dangerous, exotic, spectacular, full of violence and zealotry. That there is an overwhelming surfeit of such imagery, to the point where it numbs far more than it moves, or it excites the aesthetic senses instead of the moral ones, is a condition the information-consuming classes have had to contend with for some years now. Is it really that we don't care, or do we lack some connecting link, a spark to engage our sense of mutual responsibility? Western journalists know their audiences usually require a connection to individuals before putting emotions in gear. Big issues are often defined through the stories of selected individuals. But the voice of a newscaster or reporter remains an institutional, detached voice, and the products of news are now more like a kind of realist theater than ever. News isn't a forum in which connections can be forged. Maybe there are just too many people in the world anymore, or maybe it isn't supposed to be that at all, really. Its first job may be to make money, but I know plenty of my colleagues who wish it were such a forum and who work very hard to make it that anyway.

But all too often, it doesn't work. News from the Gaza Strip shows poverty or violence, one or the other, and preferably, these days, Muslim "fundamentalist" violence, nearly all the time. This defines Gaza, this is Gaza in the Western mind. But such a definition is a product of how one looks at the world. What do I see through my camera if I acknowledge that Gazans are, first, my human equals and, then, never just photographic *subjects* but *participants* in creating this story? What do I see if I assume Canada Camp and all of Gaza is indeed as complex a society as any other? The plains of life, the mundane, the routine and the trivial do not deny the more spectacular events that make headlines. They put the headlines into a context. Make them real again.

Several days later, Abu Sharaf says he will be happy to drive Mohammed and me to Tel el Sultan today because he nearly ended up in Canada Camp himself. His miniature, white UN Citroen registers every lump and rut from the Social Welfare Office to Tel el Sultan. The car is one of his perks as UNRWA Area Operations Officer for the southern Gaza Strip. His thick black glasses are the kind I associate with Egyptian bureaucrats, but behind them, his face is as bright as this unseasonably warm day is clear. He tells us that in 1971, when Israeli General Ariel Sharon launched the "Iron Fist" counterattack against the Palestinian resistance, he was living near the market in Rafah. When the "Sharon Streets" went in—the boulevard-sized swaths that carved the refugee camps into militarily manageable sectors—his house was among those bulldozed. He departed to live with relatives in Gaza city, where he remains.

"I thank God I did not choose to go to Canada," he says. "When it was first built, it did not appear very bad, and I almost went there. We had that choice. But my relatives near Gaza helped us avoid it. These people used to be my neighbors."

He wants to visit Abd El Rahman, an old barber, first. Abd El Rahman, he says, cut his hair from the time he was a child until 1971. We haven't called ahead: there are no telephones in

Canada Camp Palestine and besides, here, a spontaneous visit marks deeper friendship than a planned one.

Abd El Rahman grins at us from his two-chair barbershop underneath his house. He and Abu Sharaf embrace and kiss each other lightly twice on each cheek. "Welcome, welcome! How are you? Welcome!" he says, smiling broadly as Mohammed and I shake his small, wrinkled hand. When we sit, he appears eager for the honor of being the one interviewed today. He has been a barber, he says, since 1954, and he came to his present home in 1991.

"What were relations like in Egypt between the people of the camp and the Egyptians?" I ask.

Mohammed translates, and Abd El Rahman looks at the ground and seems to smirk.

"Maybe there are some stories or jokes?" I try to prompt him.

"Oh yes, there were a lot, a lot." He laughs to himself again. "The stress of the situation you know. Always about the Egyptians. But I don't know if you should write it down."

Mohammed explains we won't use his real name, and he strokes the stubble on his beard.

"In the early days of the camp, our [UN] ration food included butter. It doesn't anymore. But back then the Egyptians would look at this butter and think it must be fresh from the cow. They would taste it and say it was excellent. But we knew it came from far away, from other countries and that it was really very old. We thought it was awful. So we would give it away, and they would be so happy!" He slaps his knees with both hands.

"So there is a class difference between the camp residents and the Egyptians?"

Mohammed interjects, "Oh yes, you would not believe how great it is. You know most of the people in this part of Gaza Strip come from around Isdud [now Ashdod, Israel] and the surrounding villages, where they had farms and businesses. My own father had 100 dunums [twenty-five acres] before '48. But the Egyptians in Rafah have always been so poor. Most people in Canada Camp could be called 'intermediate' class, you know. Not the poorest, not wealthy, but people with trades and many with educations and even university certificates."

"In the first days of the border separation," Abd El Rahman continues, "some of the Egyptian soldiers gathered at my shop. I wanted to give them some food, something easy, like eggs, to please them, show some hospitality and avoid future trouble from them. One said, 'No, please, we cannot accept, because our officer told us that you Palestinians would poison food.' But another came up and yelled at him, 'No, you idiot! Please, mister, give us the food! The officer can go to hell!'"

This breaks Mohammed and Abu Sharaf up. "You know the Egyptian soldiers," Mohammed clarifies for me, "they are only paid two or maybe three dollars a month, the unfortunate men."

Abd El Rahman insists we stay for lunch, which is enormous. Later, we walk over to Mustafa's house.

He is seated on the floor, huddled with a builder over plans rolled out on a tiny table. A third man, Khaled Shinawi, is with them, a planner in Rafah's municipal offices. He is an unsmiling man with lines so deeply carved into his face they could have been done with a knife. He kneels on the carpet. He has nothing but professional disdain for Canada Camp Palestine.

"From a planner's perspective, this place is terrible," he says as Mohammed translates. "There are no playgrounds, no common areas."

"Except for all the open sand," I say.

"And what is this? Sand? This is not a proper kind of common area. Planning standards call for real streets between houses, not just this sand. A planned community should use half its land for houses, a quarter for roads and a quarter for schools, shops and other areas. But Canada is 85 percent houses. There are no plans for shops, no plans for schools. There is not even space for a mosque. And this is a community of what will be more than 6,000 people!" he exclaims. "With none of the required services here, well, this is why we still call it a camp."

"But the families do own the land they get, right?" I ask.

"It is a ninety-nine-year lease from the government. But there is a clause that states that in the event of an archeological discovery, the government can seize the land without legal process and, if they want to, demolish the house without compensation."

"So they have a way out."

He shrugs and nods, exhaling sharply.

An hour later our small group has grown into a kind of roving diplomatic delegation. Mustafa and Khaled joined Abu Sharaf, Mohammed and me for a walk, and now we are standing in the yellow, hazy light of late afternoon atop the flat roof of the tallest house in the camp, Abu Yasser's house. It was I who asked to come here for the view. From here we can see clearly the Israeli settlements of Rafiah Yam, Bedolah and Mitzpe Atzomona. None of this group, however, know these names, or will admit they do. More questions about the settlements receive shrugs and brief, uninterested answers.

At age sixty-three, Abu Yasser works as a "grade one" security guard at the Rafah UNRWA Distribution Center for emergency food rations. Born in Isdud, he is quick to say life was better on the other side. "In Canada Camp [Egypt] I could save more than half my salary. Two hundred dollars was all you needed for a month's food and expenses for the whole family in Egypt." He earns 459 U.S. dollars a month. UNRWA employees are all paid in dollars, making UNRWA jobs some of the best in the Strip.

As thick coffee appears from women downstairs, I do some quick math. He was saving $230 a month. In Canada Camp. As a security guard. But, I remember, only fifty-three people work for UNRWA in Canada Camp Egypt, where unemployment is the norm.

"Abu Yasser, you had a great job," I say. "Not many people in my country can save $230 a month! What did the people in the camp who didn't work for UNRWA think of you?"

"Oh, they were very jealous," he says, looking out over the camp, the sun gleaming from a golden dot in each eye. "They called us 'the dollar people.' They would say to us, 'You are just sitting around all the time eating kebab, eating steaks! You are spies and collaborators!'"

Four days later, I enter Canada Camp Palestine alone for the first time. It's safe, I am sure: I can recite names of those I am visiting to any suspicious passersby. Mohammed began a new job in Gaza today, and until he has a day off to accompany me next month, I'm on my own. More depressing than that, the winter rains arrived yesterday. Dirt roads have turned to sludge, and paved roads are frequently entirely submerged.

In the camp, no one is home and I don't understand why. I feel confused, conspicuous, vulnerable, lonely and very wet. Insulated no more by Mohammed's liaisons, for the first time I also feel like the outsider I really am.

Near Rowhi's house just beyond the camp I run into Hazim, a young man I'd met briefly twice before and not yet had a chance to speak with. He is on his way home from Khan Yunis Technical College, where he studies English literature.

"Why does America support Israel so much?" he inquires as we walk toward his house. "America helps people all over the world, but not the Palestinian people. Why?" He is sincere.

I have a hard time with a succinct reply. I try something about the Holocaust, about the current political clout of the American pro-Israeli lobby; the bombs and hijackings of the 1970s and 1980s that allowed "terrorist" to become a virtual suffix for "Palestinian." I finish with the role of Israel as a U.S. client state in the Middle East.

"I think the Jewish control the whole world," he replies. "Do you agree with this?" His voice is still soft, guileless.

"No. No, no," I say, raising my hands and stopping briefly in the drizzle for emphasis. "That is dangerous! The Jews have had many enemies and millions and millions of them have been killed. They are afraid of being killed again, maybe, but they do not control the whole world." I don't want to offend him by losing patience or becoming offended myself.

"But I have heard that if there is a problem in the world, any kind of problem, it is because of the Jewish?" He lifts his voice at the end to turn the statement into a question.

"No, I cannot agree with that," I say, shocked, not knowing where to begin responding. We walk the rest of the way quietly.

Hazim is an intelligent young man. His questions come from his experience. Here on the far edge of Rafah, the poorest town in the Strip with the highest percentage of refugees, the most statistically violent area of the Gaza Strip, one of the nerve centers of the *intifada*, the town he grew up in—cut off from his occupied homeland by razor wire—well, who, at age twenty-two, could find much redeeming to say about The Enemy? In Rafah, it always comes down to: they are denying us our rights; they are taking our land; they are shooting us.

Once arrived at his house, our difference of opinion seems not to matter and I'm glad. I am introduced to his mother with a polite brevity that is not lacking warmth. He lives here, he says, with only one brother, who works in Israel. His father died in 1978, in Egypt. Hazim seems lonely. We sip tea and talk about Canada Camp Egypt.

"It's more difficult to talk there because of the *mukhabarat*," he says, using the Arabic word for "intelligence," meaning the Egyptian domestic security service.

"So if you were still living there, and we met like we did today, would you feel comfortable talking like we are now?"

"I don't think so, no," he replies, and he doesn't want to talk about the *mukhabarat* any more.

At my guest apartment back in Rimal I dump lengthy accounts of these first two weeks' work on the sympathetic ear of Loren, one of my two hosts. Two years in Gaza, four years in the West Bank and several more in Cairo as a teacher of English have earned him an insight rare among foreigners. I am complaining about men. "I haven't spoken to a single Palestinian woman except for Hanan. I'm seeing only half of Gaza!"

He is stirring pasta. His advice is to give up on women at once. "Why fight to show something you won't ever be able to show in anything like the depth a female reporter could come here and show within days? But the men here," he continues with focused intensity, "men, they have their own incredibly rich and subtle system of social habits that would be so great to show, something that gets left out of everything that is ever said about Gaza because everyone is always talking about the occupation and the *intifada*. But the gestures, the visiting—"

"The handshakes—" I toss in.

"Yes, handshakes, and the way men hold children all the time, the tea, the sharing of cigarettes and the trust men give each other, the honesty in the shops here, all this. You'll never access the world of women, and unless you say this, people will think that what little you do get about women is the whole story, or sufficient, which it won't be, can't be."

"Well," I counter, "Mohammed thinks we'll interview and photograph men and women equally over the long run, because he knows them."

"OK, maybe. But in the meantime you're hanging out with men, period. Look at the way they touch each other, it's so, so—"

"You know," I say carefully, "it's like there's no 'coolness' here. I can be sincere here, say things to other men that would be sentimental or uncomfortable to say to another man back home. And you know? I totally love it."

"Yeah," he replies. "There's so much that doesn't translate really. Or it takes too long to explain. Stuff we can't ever understand about people except by sitting and listening for a long time."

CHAPTER 3
FAMILY

On the final, drizzly day of January, a Rimal grocer passes me news. Khan Yunis, where I am spending occasional nights in Mohammed's house—the closest I can live to Canada Camp—is under curfew. Guerrillas from Hamas, the acronym for Muslim Resistance Movement, ambushed three Israeli soldiers outside Khan Yunis last night. Two were killed. I was supposed to meet Mohammed at home late this afternoon.

Even after two weeks here in Gaza, I find I can take the news with equanimity. It is all too easy here to let the political replace the natural, as if I were being delayed by bad weather. Outrage at collective punishments—curfew is a violation of the Fourth Geneva Convention—can't be summoned up every time they occur or I'd be worn out in no time. Ever since Israel stonewalled the December 18, 1992, UN Security Council order to return 415 Palestinian men expelled for alleged advocacy of a Muslim theocracy in all Israel-Palestine, the ante of conflict has been rising steadily in the Strip. Fewer stones in the air these days. More guns, although the match is hardly equal: In the month and a half since December 1, Gazans dead from Israeli security forces number twenty-seven; from the preceding July to November, seventeen were killed. Nearly all were unarmed. Injured Gazans since December total a shocking 1,915. In contrast, four Israelis were stabbed by a Gazan in the Tel Aviv bus station two weeks ago, and a policeman was killed just before the 415 were expelled.

In my brief exchange with the grocer, the plodding Washington peace talks don't come up. Of course not. They never do. In Gaza, it's as if they don't exist. What exists here now are street posters of the four major armed factions—two

An ordinary evening meal at Mohammed's house.

secular and two Islamist—on lampposts and walls everywhere.
Boys speak the names with respect, as they would sports teams
in safer lands. Hawks. Eagles. Qassam. Jihad.

I phone Mohammed's house. Khan Yunis has far more telephone lines than Rafah. His mother answers and chides me in
simplified Arabic like I'm an errant boy: "No, no, the curfew is
over now! Yes, it's over. Where are you? Gaza? You come to this
house, this is your house! No problem! No army!" I promise
her I'll be there in a couple of hours. What welcome could be
warmer?

The road south is clear, meaning no checkpoints, except
the one at Kfar Darom, Israel's only settlement along the main
highway, where soldiers in a watchtower wave cars by one at a
time but they don't check ID's. This highway has paved one of
the oldest roads in the world. Ancient Egyptians called it The
Horus Road, Romans named it Via Maris, and to Israel it goes
as Route Four. Along this coastal highway passed most of the
caravan trade between Africa and Asia for 4,000 years. Long
before that trade, it may have been this way that some of the
earliest of humans made their way out of Africa to found the
civilizations of the Fertile Crescent.

Although Gaza always was the main regional trading center, the Egyptian Mamluk sultans of the fourteenth century
found it useful to provide travelers an additional hostelry south
along this road. Khan Yunis grew around its *khan*, which resem-
bled a castle but served as a caravan hotel, market and central
mosque. The scant remains of the *khan* dedicated in 1387 to
Yunis Ibn Abdullah an-Nawruzi ad-Dawadar now crumble
slowly in the main square, long ago eclipsed in public significance by the modern mosque with its seventy-five-foot minaret,
which is today topped by an illegal Palestinian flag.

Downtown Khan Yunis is darker and more claustrophobic
than Gaza city. The streets run mucky with a mixture of rain-
water and errant sewage regardless of the weather. Horse and
donkey carts mix equally with cars, and electric wires swoop
overhead, the tangled rigging of a shipwreck town. From the
taxi stand it is two blocks to Mohammed's house.

I walk alone, casually slinging a camera around my neck to signal my business. Without it, I fear my bulky equipment bag might look suspicious. But I don't use the camera, not without permission, ever. The sidewalks are packed with men walking or sitting outside shops that seem to put as many of their wares as possible outside, too. I pass close by them, as the way is narrow, briefly entering that social distance where anonymity is inappropriate. I return their greetings or offer greetings myself, not missing a chance to make contact, however brief. Occasionally I pause long enough to shake hands and turn down tea, saying I must visit my friend. There is no hurry. This may be a city of more than 80,000 people, but in its soul it is a place for a village walking style. This is the opposite of my far more familiar photographer's urban walking strategy: don't look anyone in the eyes; walk without pause; stay anonymous.

Mohammed's family home is on the near edge of the camp, which after forty-five years now blends almost seamlessly with the town. The house is a one-story, cinder block building with corrugated roofing. It's only two-thirds its original size, as several rooms were lost to Israeli bulldozers when the "Sharon Street" it now sits on came along in the mid-1970s. Seven adults and eight children live here. More friends or relatives may be visiting at any time. Drying laundry splashes color on the otherwise drab outside. A smear of sewage meanders down the left side of the street past the house. Kids spot my camera and react with bursts of "Hallo!" and "What is your name!" and "*Sawwerna!*", "Take our picture!" Always the same words, the same demand, over and over. I smile, wave, and walk on, a one-man parade.

By now I've visited quite a few times, and I go in the back way. This I find abutting the street, through a red curtain and a vestibule-like pantry of salvaged corrugated metal. Mohammed's older brother threw the pantry together early in the *intifada*, he told me, not to add space to the house so much as to deflect Israeli tear gas canisters before they hit the house proper. He built slits in the metal so that while confrontations were happening up the street, the family could watch for soldiers without being seen.

Using this door makes me feel like I belong. My relationship with Mohammed crossed over, at some time this week, into real friendship. We liked each other from the morning we met last summer, and he trusted me at once due to a coincidental mutual friend in the U.S. To him I was never entirely a stranger. Since that day our conversations branch like trees despite the wild differences in the outer circumstances of our lives. I respect how he doesn't dwell on politics; how he's critical of his society, when warranted, in front of a foreigner; how he wishes, he said once, he could speak to Israelis other than soldiers, to find out what they are really like. I've come to rely on his judgment, and he seems to be able to dissipate his own stress skillfully with an easy, infectious laugh. I'm not the only one who likes him: his living room is always full of pre-curfew evening visitors. For his part, he's told me he respects my approach to his friends and countrymen, as well as my intentions for the Canada Camp story. On that project, we've agreed, we're full partners now.

I greet his mother by smiling and raising my hand, not shaking hands anymore—too formal. She wears black every day, except for the brilliant white *hijab*, or head scarf, a wrap that in the Gaza Strip seems thinner and more gauze-like than anywhere I've seen. It flows all the way to her waist. A few gray hairs escape from underneath, and she is barefoot despite the cold tile floor. Her husband—Mohammed's father—died a few months before Mohammed and I met last summer. She tells me Mohammed isn't home yet. I don't see Ibtisam, Mohammed's wife, anywhere, so I join seventeen-year-old Rafat, the youngest of Mohammed's four brothers, and a handful of his friends in another room around a charcoal brazier, the only heat in the house. The friends launch insistent questions in Arabic, the kind that help them fix me on their mental maps of reality.

"Which is better, Gaza or America?" one asks.

"OK," I grin, pausing to arrange a sequence of Arabic words while not taking this too seriously, "you've seen American TV. But the important thing is to know that everywhere there are good people, and bad people. Gaza and America."

"Why does America do one thing against Iraq but not the same against Israel?" says another, referring to the January air raid on Baghdad hours after a UN deadline passed, and the simultaneous lack of enforcement to UN Resolution 799 mandating the return of expelled Palestinian Muslim leaders.

"Politics, you know," I say. "I think it is wrong, but that is the American government and Israel." I don't know the word for "hypocrisy" in Arabic.

"How do you feel when you see an Israeli soldier kill a Palestinian child?" interrupts another, more declarative than interrogatory. I dump him a look that back home would clearly say, "Give me a break," but I'm not sure what he reads.

Mohammed walks in and at once I feel like a pupil whose pop quiz is cut short by the bell. He's hungry, exhausted, wet, and holding his forehead. It's raining now, he says. He's carrying a cake in a cardboard box, drooping now from the rain, tied with string. Today is his and Ibtisam's fourth anniversary.

"You would not believe it, Dick," he says, keeping his coat on against the chill and hugging the small children who run up to him. He hides the surprise cake on a shelf. "I had to mediate in three confrontations today, two in Jabalia and one in Beach Camp," he says. "It was so bad. We saw many, many injured. And then they had a special checkpoint near Nuseirat Camp, and I had to stand in the rain for a taxi right next to all the soldiers."

I ask about the confrontations, but he doesn't want to go into details, preferring to hold kids and smoke a cigarette. Since he left the Social Welfare Office a week ago, his new job title is that of Refugee Affairs Assistant. He spends the day in a UN car as translator and guide for one of eight Refugee Affairs Officers, or RAOs. Each RAO is European or North American, on a one-year contract to serve as a liaison between the refugee population and UNRWA services. In practice, however, they are human-rights monitors: RAOs chase confrontations, and then, they don't just sit and watch. When possible, they get out and get in the middle to mediate amidst youths with stones and soldiers with guns. They tally injuries and keep detailed records of who did what at every incident. RAOs can't photograph on the job, nor can they offer their back seat to journalists. I find this unbearably frustrating. Instead of letting Mohammed just talk about his experiences, I tell him I'm amazed I have yet to see a *mwajaha*, or confrontation.

"You do not want this," he says, shaking his head. "They will shoot at you if they see the camera, believe me."

"The soldiers?"

"Yes. Even our own journalists now don't go near the confrontations so much. It's not like before in the *intifada*. They hate journalists so much now. Especially photojournalists. And if I go there with you, hoo!" he rolls his eyes, "it puts me in more danger than if I am with an RAO."

Eight-year-old Ahmed drags in a plastic sheet and spreads it over the thin rattan floor matting for dinner. It will protect against spills. End to end, it covers the small room so the family can sit about the perimeter foam mats. Suha, his ten-year-old sister, tells him to straighten it out better. She pushes him when he walks on it thoughtlessly; he pushes her back with a brief snarl that looks comical since he just lost his first front baby tooth. He runs back to the kitchen, evading her revenge.

Voices quicken, and the room grows crowded as the family gathers. With their younger brothers Sharaf, five, and Sherif, four, Ahmed and Suha begin a procession of bowls: beans with olive oil, fried potatoes, fresh tomatoes, olives, jam, and beef with gravy and bits of potato. Suha supervises the placement of the dozen-odd bowls on the mat. Aysha, their mother and Mohammed's sister-in-law, brings fresh bread stacked like Frisbees, which she warms one by one on the smokeless charcoal brazier. She keeps her scarf on when I am visiting still, as does Mohammed's mother, but Mohammed's wife Ibtisam, being younger and more liberal, doesn't. Ibtisam carries in two more bowls of beef and shoos her two sons, Hosam and Salah, ages three and two respectively, who wander about soliciting what attention they can. Mohammed holds their infant daughter, Majd.

Duties finished, Sherif climbs over to my side as all fifteen members of the family gather loosely about the meal. He and the other kids have begun calling me "Uncle Dick" now. I share my hot bread with him. Talk subsides as hands plunge torn bits of bread into this bowl and that, scooping contents by splitting the bread and folding it slightly into a modified cone shape. I've come to like eating this way: no table or individual place settings to separate people; kids free to be touched or held or instructed; and the bread warm and sensual on cold fingers.

I'm grateful for a temporary sensation of normality. Now that Rafat's friends have left, I'm nobody special anymore. With the cloak of the observer off, I let bits of conversation float about me half-understood. I don't want to do interviews here: I just want to be normal, whatever that is on the terms of this family.

Across the room, Khaled, Mohammed's second youngest brother, is grinning madly, kidding Ibtisam about something. At twenty-three, his body fairly ripples with energy; he returned recently from two years in prison, and in two weeks, he will be married. I don't understand his joke, but Ibtisam's face bursts with a laugh so big she nearly chokes. Her smile lifts her face and for a moment the solemn weight of raising an infant and two toddlers in Khan Yunis Camp falls away, or so I imagine. The sound of laughter eases my own tension from the day like medicine.

Mohammed parades out the anniversary cake. It's from Arafat's, the best bakery in Gaza, he says. A fire-engine red heart floats amidst the decorator's white fluff: it looks like an embroidered doily. I propose the heart be divided between the anniversary couple. They laugh and don't do it. Mohammed has told me theirs was one of few marriages of choice since the *intifada* reinforced the social conservatism that was already characteristic in Gazan culture. The two met as students at Birzeit University in the more liberal West Bank. There they were lucky to graduate a week before the *intifada* began in

December 1987; following Israeli closures of the university, the next class did not receive diplomas until 1992. Now, all but a handful of marriages in the Strip are arranged. We eat cake with our fingers off paper napkins around the brazier's dying coals, blankets piled over our legs, runny frosting dripping on the floor. Hosam and Salah, Mohammed's sons, smear most of their cake on their faces and hands. Nobody stops them.

Rateb, Mohammed's older brother, has been nearly silent through the meal. He is a quiet man anyway, with a soft voice. He also is one of few who don't smoke. Last week he was laid off from his job in a juice canning factory in Rehovot, Israel, a half hour north of the Erez checkpoint. He'd been a day laborer for seventeen years, and his father had also worked there before his death. Rateb supervised two Jewish men— who earned twice his wage—while maintaining the plant's hydraulic equipment. He wasn't laid off because he is Palestinian, he had been quick to explain. The factory closed. Jews and Palestinians both went, although only the former got severance pay and unemployment benefits.

Mohammed interrupts his solitude by asking how he is.

"Thanks be to God," he says without enthusiasm, the same way I would say, "Fine" if I was depressed and not eager to let on. His words, 'ham'delulah, have no exact English equivalent; it is the conventional response to "How are you?"

"What happened today?" Mohammed asks.

"You know, one place to the other, all in the rain." He pauses, expressionless. "Nobody wants anyone from Gaza any-more. I tell them I am from Gaza and they say no, no, get out, no." He looks at me, "They think we are all just terrorists now."

"You were in Israel?" I clarify.

"Yes. Factory to factory. More than twenty shekels on buses and taxis. The whole week has been this way."

"What about the letter?" I ask. The day after he was laid off, I typed a letter of recommendation for him in English. His Jewish boss, whom Rateb thought highly of, had offered to

In Tel el Sultan, a man holds permission papers, which must be renewed quarterly, to enter Israel as a day worker. To pass the border, each man must also present a magnetic ID card and a military ID card. The crossing can take up to three hours each morning. They will wake at 3:30 A.M. and return home between 7:00 and 8:00 P.M. Their labor will build an apartment building in Ashdod. Their daily wage is statistically average: U.S. $25 equivalent with no benefits. At the time this photograph was taken, two-thirds of employed Gazans worked this way.

sign any letter Rateb brought in, just to try and help him out after seventeen years of work.

"Mostly I don't even get to show it. They don't ask about other work I've done, they just don't want anyone from Gaza. A Jew gets stabbed somewhere now, and it's always one from Gaza who does it. When there is a curfew here, they get angry because I can't come to work. When there is a strike, the same thing. And now it's maybe half the days I can't go because of the situation."

Mohammed explains further, "Even though a worker from Gaza—or the West Bank—even though he is paid only half of what the Israeli man is paid, now there are not so many benefits to the company to hire Gaza workers, because the workers cannot get to Israel in the curfew or the strike."

"Even people who knew me before," Rateb says, "some of the good Israeli men who said before if I ever needed a job to come to them, they don't want anyone from Gaza anymore either. They say, 'I'm sorry, but it's too much risk.'"

I nod slowly. "Will you go back tomorrow?"

"God willing."

Meaning, I presume, yes.

In the night it rains on, anarchic crescendos of pindrops driven by a hard sea bluster. I sleep on a floor mat in long underwear, pants, shirt, wool sweater, wool socks and five blankets, a guest in the room shared already by Khaled and Rafat. Cinder blocks, I am finding, make bad insulation. A waterfall of cold air spills from a poorly shuttered window above. I feel I am indeed camping, here in Khan Yunis Camp. Forty-five winters it's been like this here. The curfewed streets outside stay silent through a thick, grudging dawn.

By 6:30 I'm sitting at the edge of another floor mattress in Mohammed and Ibtisam's bedroom, waiting to share breakfast with a bleary-eyed Mohammed. Ibtisam has been up a while, but it was Mohammed, she says, who took care of sleepless, two-year-old Salah all night. Each family in the house sleeps in one room. The Israeli morning news is on their small color television, but all I understand are rain clouds on the weather map. Mohammed is listening from beneath his blankets to Radio Monte Carlo, the standard radio news source in the Strip, broadcast all the way from tiny Monaco. Ibtisam brings a tray with a straight-handled aluminum teapot, three little glasses, a disk of bread, some cheese and a piece of last night's cake and goes to nurse baby Majd. I hand her a portion of the cake, warning her Mohammed and I will devour it all otherwise. I flip the small electric heater on its back and warm the bread on it. My head feels thick, even after two glasses of the syrupy tea. Just one night with the voices of fifteen people echoing off concrete walls wears me out.

For this morning we scheduled an interview about Canada Camp with an urban planner in the Rafah municipal offices. But there is bad news from Rafah now: three of the Red Eagles, the armed wing of the PFLP (Popular Front for the Liberation of Palestine), the quasi-socialist faction, entered the offices yesterday. A shot was fired, someone was wounded, and the offices may be closed today. I say to Mohammed we should go anyway. He nods, weary. We can call down there after eight, he says. I carry my tea into the empty living room to write notes until then. He falls back asleep.

CHAPTER 4
AMONG MEN

The Rafah municipal building is indeed open. Through a crowd of men we are escorted up to a dim, chilly, president's office. The rain knocked out electricity last night and it's not fixed yet. No one takes off his coat. Hot tea appears to smolder in the dampness. We are supposed to cover building regulations in Tel el Sultan today, but *el wadd'a*, the situation, takes over: The morning is spent mostly on urgent politics.

Witnesses to yesterday's shooting tell us three members of the PFLP Red Eagles—masked as always to prevent identification by collaborators—walked into the storefront offices and grabbed a man, an electrician. They dragged him to the street, pressed a pistol to his thigh and fired. They let him fall to the pavement. They collared another man, and he fainted at the sight of the first man's wound. They left the second man without shooting and fled. With Mohammed's translation, I understand the witnesses interpret this as part of several inter-related trends: a breakdown of discipline in the *intifada* resistance, a growing political desperation and an intensified competition among the factions for control of everything from municipal councils to charities.

"What we see in the streets now is a foggy kind of conflict," said one. "It's holding back a real revolution anymore."

The problem, they continue, is that the Rafah municipal government has lately been increasingly dominated by Fateh, Yasser Arafat's wing of the PLO. Despite their powers being limited to rubber-stamping Israeli military directives regarding utilities, sanitation and licensing, the skeletal political body is nonetheless regarded as an important local symbol of power distribution. Along with Gaza, Khan Yunis and Deir al Balah, it is one of four such councils in the Strip. As the *intifada* has dragged on, Gazans have found their sacrifices have raised their collective self-esteem but not their material or political lot; in nearly every observable respect things are now worse than in 1987. It seems that the stress that comes with a growing fear of political failure has collapsed the unity that characterized relations among political factions in the first years of the *intifada*. For some time now, the gap between moderates and militants has been widening; each day the Washington talks adjourn barren, the latter gain ground. As Fateh, which largely defines the moderate stance, draws its circle tighter against the siege, power-sharing increasingly looks like political suicide. This only heightens resentment: the shooting yesterday was, the witnesses say, simply a gangland-style warning to hire more PFLP affiliates in the municipality. Under occupation, no electoral process or judicial system permits a legitimate outlet for dissent in Palestinian society. Thus, both the paternalistic structure of the PLO and the occupation together reinforce an autocratic politics of patronage. That the internecine rivalries may be further cultivated by Israeli intelligence is, Mohammed says, a nearly universal belief, one in keeping with the ancient principle that the divided opponent is the more easily ruled.

Their tale, I realize, hints at why Mustafa, in our conversation at the Rafah Social Welfare Office, said with such emphasis he felt like a stranger in the Gaza Strip. The Canada Camp repatriates have not just entered an occupation; they have come into an underlying political scene as Byzantine and volatile as that of any oppressed nation where political discourse has been forced underground.

"Do you want to visit the man who was shot?" Mohammed asks when it seems the interview is ending.

Of course I do. We jog out into a thick, drenching rain, hugging the broken sidewalk, sheltered slightly by ragged metal awnings. At an open door, we duck in. The living room is dark and smoky, filled with several dozen men sitting on plastic chairs and tiny wicker stools about the perimeter. Some wear business suits. From the shoulders of others flow the full-

Mohammed and Omar as we walk through Khan Yunis Camp to visit another friend who has invited us for coffee and a video. Handholding between men during a good conversation is a common, casual sign of friendship.

length *jalabeeya*. Still others wear work overalls. On a couch in the corner, the wounded man is lying wrapped in blankets, his head propped on three pillows. He is dragging hard on a cigarette through a broad, opiated grin. He seems to be basking in the attention. We go to him and shake his beefy, plumber's hand, or maybe his heavy-equipment-operator's hand.

"*Salamtak*," I say, "Health be with you." Mohammed does the same. Everyone stares at me, but my appearance with Mohammed is a kind of security clearance. We shake hands all down the line of seated men, like a receiving line, saying to each one "Welcome," "Hello," "Peace be upon you" in varying combinations until we reach a pair of empty stools. Other men arrive and do the same. Others get up and leave. Trays of tea are hustled in like a busy cafe, but most men sit silently. It is a quiet, informal rite of healing, a medicine of presence and visitation. I speak these thoughts to Mohammed.

"Just wait until tonight," he whispers back, "between five and six-thirty. You won't be able to find him in this room there will be so many."

"What about the men who shot him?" I ask. "What will be done? Will anyone want revenge?"

"We hope not. There will be some to talk to the masked ones, some of the older and respected ones. This is the best way now, the only way, to deal with the problem through the community itself. We hope they can talk to the masked ones. They will have to make some amends to this man here. I don't know how. Do you want to ask him any questions?"

No one else is conversing with him. I sense if I do, the attention in the room would be deflected away from him and toward me. It doesn't feel right. "No," I reply. "I think we are here for support, human to human, not for an interview." Mohammed agrees, and I sense he made the offer out of obligation, and that he is relieved at my having declined. We stay only a few minutes, and we shake the man's hand again as we depart. He nods and thanks us, still smoking, still smiling.

"You know," Mohammed says as we search out a taxi in the downpour, "this ritual is also done every time someone comes back from prison. When Khaled—my brother—came back a few months ago from two years in prison, maybe 500 people came to the house to greet him. And my brother-in-law, the one who was almost expelled by Israel last summer, when he came back, you would not believe it, but people came for several days from all over Gaza Strip and even from the West Bank to greet him."

The rain has eased to a fine mist by afternoon. A friend of Mohammed's, Ahmed, escorts me through Khan Yunis Camp to the house of another friend, Omar, where I agreed a week ago to spend two days as a wedding photographer. I hadn't been sure this was a good idea at first, sensing I ought to seek out weddings in Tel el Sultan instead. Mohammed had shaken his head. "Everyone will be there, even some from Canada Camp, and all of my friends. It will be good for your relations." He said it as if it was so obvious. I hoped my hesitation hadn't offended him.

Ahmed walks in loping but passionless strides, as if there was some contradiction between the demands of his six-foot-plus frame and his state of mind. He hunches to speak to me in a voice that with years could carry authority. He is twenty-three, and he is majoring in English at the Islamic University in Gaza city, which he hates, he hastens to add, because he is a socialist. It is, however, the only university in the Gaza Strip. He can tell me his politics, he says, because he spent two years in Israel's Ketziot prison in the Negev desert, and thus the authorities are aware of his formerly activist stance. Prison, too, was his education: within the fifty-man tents there is what some wryly call Palestine's shadow educational system, *jama'it al sijin*, "prison university." His eyes appear to burn; his face is drawn and clearly not accustomed to laughter as is Mohammed's. Still, his manner is so gentle I wonder if I am just reading his features all wrong. I like him at once. He finds us a Peugeot jalopy on one of those absurd expanses of pavement that could land aircraft, Sea Street, a "Sharon Street."

At Omar's house, a sand yard is fenced by twisted chunks of corrugated scrap metal, car hoods and barbed wire. Chickens huddle in a corner. The one-story, cinder-block house is packed with *shabab*, young men in their late teens and twenties, nearly all in black vinyl jackets like fashion uniforms, singing to a drum and tambourine. No women. I drop my overnight bag in the room Omar will share with his bride. It gleams with layers of fresh-smelling, glossy white paint. Three fluorescent tubes glare off the new bedroom set: the bed with end tables built in; the mirrored dresser and the long, standing wardrobe for the house without closets. Everything is white. It has been Omar's duty as groom to prepare this, and his diligence in carrying out the ritual task has been watched carefully by his bride's father. In a better time and place, he would have readied a whole house.

Omar grips my hand and hustles me through the crowd, making rapid introductions I will never remember. His black hair is combed slick, and he wears a thin black tie under a black jacket. His manner is gracious, subtly bespeaking an upbringing for which this house and camp are obviously unsuitable. In a moment we are somehow outside again in a small crowd, now heaving his friend Musa's pea-green stretch Mercedes taxi out of axle-deep mud. That done, Omar holds open the door and insists I take the front seat as guest of honor. Ahmed, who has followed me silently like a bodyguard, sits in back with Omar. We pile through dusky, rock-strewn alleys of the camp, some paved, some not, swerving around stray cinder blocks, mudholes and children. Musa and Omar converse so loudly, so sharply and rapidly, I feel immediately shell-shocked: they sound furious, as if they've had too much espresso and now they are about to come to blows. But this is fun, wild fun. I have no idea where we are, or even why we are in the car.

"Hallu Dick! How are you!" Musa hollers, his boyish face dimpled and beaming like he just opened a present, eyes gaping.

I try to match his vocal assault, "Great! Good! Where are we going?"

"Film! For you! For the wedding! But we must hurry because of curfew!"

We careen up another dirt road and splash our way to the far edge of the camp, where Israeli army watchtowers dot the sand beyond. Here among the shops is, of all things, a photo studio. Omar buys four rolls and drops them in my hand.

Back at the house, the room of *shabab* throbs to the drum, tambourine and fifty pairs of hands clapping. Omar rushes the pictures—curfew, he reminds me—smoothing his hair again and wiggling through the crowd, grabbing men with whom he wants to be photographed. After a dozen-odd flash pops, he hauls me next door to his immediate family.

I step into another world. Men and women sit together, something I have experienced only at Mohammed's. Voices high and low mingle in the air. Omar jumps from one person to the next, trying to keep his smile as natural as he can under the pressure of the curfew now in ten minutes. Done, he shuttles me out as quickly as we entered, back to the other house. The real wedding will be tomorrow, he says; tonight is just the party for his family. The bride's family has their own party tonight, too. Tomorrow they will celebrate together.

Just before curfew I am surrounded by *shabab* who find a live foreign photographer far more interesting than one final round of song. It's a twenty-man interview, and I answer anyone who can make his question heard above the others. My answers don't stand a chance in the verbal stampede, but I try, in order to be polite, ignoring aggressive tugs on my jacket and point-blank shouts to "Listen! Listen!" Clinton-Rabin-Bush, prison-Israel-no work, occupation-*intifada*-Palestine, America, America, yes, I am married, no, no children but with the help of God next year. We're conversation-surfing, tumbling together, scanning a vast social territory too hastily, but it's all we have. In minutes, someone announces seven o'clock. The evening falls flat, like someone just unplugged it. Everyone leaves at once. The house is now silent. I take a deep breath, and only Omar remains. I accept his invitation to dinner next door at his brother Abu Eyad's.

All furniture has been cleared out of the living room except for a television playing crooning Egyptian and Syrian music videos. Men of all ages sit around the perimeter on mats. Everyone will spend the night here; some may sleep. I spot Mohammed, finished now with his afternoon shift. We sit together.

One aggressive youth accosts me, interrupting, poking, talking loudly in English as bad as my Arabic, "Listen! What you think of this?! What about our situation?! You know Gamel Abdel Nasser? That is my name, Nasser!" He carries on like a truck with a stuck throttle, and Mohammed politely quiets him by pulling me away to introduce me to two saucer-eyed young men who, Mohammed says, are studying English, like Ahmed. I am the first foreigner they have ever conversed with in English. They are dressed nearly identically. With bicycles they could pass as Mormon missionaries. I am astounded they are reading Macbeth—in English—in only their second year. They lean forward, intent on eye contact to help them speak what has been, for them, a written language.

Food interrupts us, waves of it, all imported from the women's party next door. Beans, hummus, tomatoes mixed with spiced potatoes, cauliflower and armloads of hot bread, but no meat: an ox will be slaughtered tonight for tomorrow's feast. The room grows quiet as we eat. I tilt toward Nasser and kid him, "Hey Nasser! Why don't you say something? You're too quiet and it's no good anymore!" I overplay a grin to make sure he knows I'm joking in my simple Arabic. His mouth is stuffed like a chipmunk. He chokes on a laugh and swings me a stiff, stinging high-five. He is obnoxious but funny; I hope he at least thinks the same of me.

The English students consult each other before each statement, so I feel like I am really talking to one person. "Who is your favorite singer?" I ask, glancing at the video.

They look at me and shake their heads, and one clucks and says, "haraam."

"Forbidden?" I reply in English.

"Yes, in our religion, you know, music is forbidden. It takes you away from the Qur'an."

I am puzzled. I've never heard this interpretation in Islam. "But I've even visited a rally of Hamas once," I say, "and even they had music. Powerful drumming."

"This is different. This is for *jihad*."

To translate this word exclusively as "holy war" is something of a semantic error: it means "struggle for righteousness," which, in its highest form, is understood first as a personal affair, a struggle for self-discipline through fasting, prayer or "right action." Only then can its parallel, political dimension be undertaken properly.

"So all the famous Arab singers, Fairouz, Um Khalsoum, Abdul Wahab, they would be forbidden by a Palestinian Islamic state?" I can't believe they would imply this: these performers are regarded as defining the heart and soul of modern Arab culture.

"Yes," one says as they both nod, their faces unchanging in gentle, callow sincerity.

Mohammed rolls his eyes and says in a quiet aside, "You know they are just saying this because that is what they are told at the Islamic University. Some professors are so strict there. But not all. What they really would forbid is music with women's voices. Don't take them seriously, please."

I shift the subject back to Macbeth, but Abu Eyad, Omar's eldest brother and our host, wants to greet his foreign guest. He looks old enough to be Omar's father; I can't guess his age.

"Why don't the American people support the Palestinian cause? Why help Israel so much?" he fires, bluntly, before even finishing our long handshake.

I try not to recoil visibly. A detailed opinion, I decide, might best respect his hospitality. "There is a long history of conflict between the Arabs and the West," I finish after several minutes. "Fear and discrimination today is directed not only against Palestinians."

He raises one finger at me didactically. We are sitting cross-legged, facing each other, our knees nearly touching. "The West is not against the Arab, but against the Muslim! All the world must become Muslim!" he proclaims. "All people will return to Allah anyway! The Qur'an is from God, directly in the Arabic language, not like the book of the Jews and Christians that has been changed and rewritten!"

He carries on in this vein, and I grow irritated. Although his theology is proper within Islam, in the context of his present oppression by one "chosen people," his counter-declarations of divinely select status seem at best ironic and, at worst, like a symptom of abused mimicking abuser. But Abu Eyad is our host. After some consideration, I risk equivalent bluntness padded with diplomacy.

"Abu Eyad," I insert into a pause, raising my hand, "because I am your guest and we have eaten this delicious meal, you have accepted me as a friend, and so I will speak as freely as you do with me. I do not agree with any of this. I am a Christian and I do not need to become Muslim. Heaven to me is a large room with many, perhaps thousands, of doors. To say there is only one door can only bring us all more war."

"The wars come from the other religions that do not know the Qur'an," he says loudly for emphasis, waving his finger again. "But we can live with the Jews and the others. If they only leave us alone, then we will leave them alone."

Mohammed, bless him, tells Abu Eyad he has tired of translating, and he and I must rise early tomorrow. I am exhausted, too. Abu Eyad and I shake hands longer and harder than I expected we might. In another room, Mohammed and I pull out foam mats and blankets where other men lie already.

"You know he speaks this way because he really likes you," Mohammed explains later.

"Chauvinism is chauvinism," I reply, too worn out for intercultural understanding.

"He is venting frustration. He wants to make sure you know what happened to him from his point of view. If people were not suffering so, they would not be talking about religion in this way, believe me. It is like a transference, you know? Rights denied, land stolen. Under such stress as we have we cannot be expected to be rational always."

"So how do you do it?"

"I do not always, absolutely not. This is our life."

I finish notes by flashlight. From the main room, conversation pounds the night until dawn.

I slip out of the house early, telling Mohammed I'll be back in time for the afternoon feast. As I leave, I see early-rising women silently sorting the giant pots that will cook for more than 200. The first sunlight in a week slices color and shadow amidst the camp buildings where few lines run true or unbroken. An exodus of children walks on Sea Street toward the schools, into the sun, the white scarves of the girls edged in saffron.

The roads have been so flooded lately I've allowed two hours for this twenty-mile journey to Gaza for an interview that will, I hope, secure my permission to enter Canada Camp Egypt in two weeks. But today there are more problems than water. Outside Khan Yunis, nearly a hundred cars are massed in front of the Kfar Darom checkpoint. Like a scene in any rush hour crunch, the man next to me keeps looking at his watch and thumping his hand on the windowsill.

The driver gives up and about-faces our taxi. We aren't alone, and we join a caravan of dozens on a creeping, backroad run around the checkpoint, grinding and squishing along a one-lane track, potholes like mortar craters, orange trees and cactuses scratching paint on both sides, all the way into Deir al Balah. When we return to the highway, two army jeeps have stopped traffic again. Two Peugeot taxis are off to the right, doors and trunks open. A dozen men stand in line, heads down, hands clasped in front. Their pose is humiliating, a forced penitence. A soldier stands watch on them, gun pointed. I want to sneak a photo, but I can't see all the soldiers and I don't want to endanger other passengers if a soldier spots me and stops us, too. The old man behind me shakes his head and mutters as he watches, "God help them, God help them." A soldier waves and untangles the traffic.

A few minutes later, a third delay slows us. The driver, now visibly furious, blows his cigarette smoke out hard. It's another

of what Gazans satirically call *zaffeh*, a "wedding procession."
An army jeep is playing mother duck to our line of several
dozen cars, creeping down the road at twenty mph. It's illegal
to pass the jeep, and the penalty for violation is clear: a soldier
keeps a heavy, mounted machine gun aimed at the lead car.
I've gotten used to this: since December, jeeps have plied the
highway at these slow speeds, mostly for harassment, people
say. The no-passing rule, however, does not apply to Jewish
settlers' cars, which zip past us sporting Israeli yellow license
plates. Palestinian cars in Gaza bear white plates.

Cresting a hill, the jeep turns off at a sandbagged army
post. Our driver dives right, down onto the sloping, soggy
shoulder, pumps up our speed and puts the entire procession
behind us in a gravel-spitting, brilliantly skillful, Hollywood
maneuver. At the checkpoint, we weave clear of the army's
three concrete barrier cubes, power back up to eighty mph on
an open road, and beyond the flat, broad fields, rows of palm
trees burst like flowers in the morning sun.

I'm early back to the wedding lunch, and happy. My clearance
into Canada Camp Egypt is set. Before the feast, Ahmed offers
to take me on a walk through the camp. Musa joins us. He
and Ahmed are good friends, sort of a Mutt and Jeff team.
Musa has eight children; Ahmed is single. Musa's face is explo-
sive with expression; Ahmed is impassive. We walk toward
Ahmed's house. Only laundry and graffiti bring discernible
colors to the long streets of cinder-block homes. Sewage trick-
les and puddles where children play barefoot. At the edge of
the camp, an Israeli army watchtower rises in the sand, guard-
ing the Jewish settlement of Qatif beyond. It looks like a
prison tower.

We stand and stare at it, much as we might gaze out over a
river from the edge of any city in the world.

"So, Ahmed, what are you going to do?" I begin, remembering he, unlike Mohammed, can talk politics because he's
been to prison.

"I really don't know," he replies. "Really I don't. We must fight to get them to leave, to get back our land."

"Dick," Musa says, "my father had 100 dunums [twenty-five acres] near Isdud before '48. Now it is Israel. I am here. We have to liberate the land. It is Palestine. They stole it. And now they are trying to steal it here, too, right here in Gaza Strip!"

"So how can you actually liberate it?" I ask. "The idea of Arabs joining a war against Israel is far in the past, it's—"

"But this is the only way," says Ahmed.

"But the Arabs have treated you as badly as Israel sometimes, you know this!"

"I know. But what else is there?"

"Would you support two states?"

"What, and leave us here in Gaza?" Ahmed says with more than a touch of incredulity. "Two states might not be so bad for people in the West Bank, but for us, there are too many of us here. We need land. We need our land back. Gaza is too small."

"Yes," says Musa, "and the Arab countries must help."

"But Abu Ammar [Yasser Arafat] supported Saddam Hussein two years ago and destroyed the Palestinian relationship with the Gulf Arabs! They won't ever help now," I say, enjoying the trust that comes from a sincere argument.

"It is our only hope for our land," says Musa.

"Even if they did," I continue, "the Arab armies would be defeated by the United States."

"No," says Ahmed, as if nailing the word to a wooden door. "The Arab armies would be victorious."

"How?"

"Because the Arab fighters are better. They would be fighting for their homeland, for justice."

As our conversation continues, I notice just as there is no talk of the Washington peace talks, so is there no talk of the *intifada*. Has it become a constant, a way of life, an attitude more than a political strategy, something taken for granted and thus not even a topic of conversation? Or is it increasingly moribund, unable to overcome the repressive reactions it inspired from Israel, its tactics of strikes and stonings now still painful but politically impotent gestures?

At the wedding meal, Omar is carefully keeping mud off his polished shoes. He is very disappointed, he tells me when he takes me aside. His father-in-law, a religious man, has declared he wants no photographs in the wedding house made by any-one outside the family. The problem is, no one inside the family has a camera. I hand him the film he bought along with a pocket camera I always carry. "Return it when you can," I say. He thanks me, apologizes for disinviting me, and disappears.

I confine myself to Abu Eyad's house, where the crowd of male friends, colleagues and distant relatives is huge. We pack full every room and spill out into the yard, all sitting on wicker stools rented for the day. There must be 250 of us. A bucket brigade of *shabab* loudly hustles in aluminum platter after alu-minum platter, each the size of a large pizza. From each rises a conical mound of golden saffron rice, topped with fist-sized chunks of ox meat. Inside, we sit four or five to a platter. The young boys jump through the crowd, handing each man a big steel spoon and a bottle of cola or 7-Up, no requests, just take what's handed your way. I sit with Ahmed. Mohammed, off work just in time, joins us, coat still on. The rice is laced with roasted almonds and garlic cloves; it is delicious. Our collec-tive eating is furious. Mohammed and a man to my right harass me to eat more and more. I indulge them, tearing at the meat with my fingers and putting away more of the platter than the others, perfect guest's etiquette. Ahmed seems detached, above the kidding. In less than thirty minutes, it's all over. We wash up at a faucet outside, the boys begin stacking stools, and the men drift away.

Mohammed and I part, too. He goes back home, and I leave for the East Jerusalem photo lab. When I return, he reminds me, he'll have a few days off, and we'll spend two days and nights in Canada Camp Palestine.

CHAPTER 5
CONFLICTS

Mohammed looks tired this afternoon. In a subdued voice he still agrees yes, okay, we must go to Canada Camp as planned. He says his nose is stuffed up. He fears a cold. Then without shifting tone he adds that he and his RAO spent the morning in a "terrifying" confrontation in Jabalia camp. "We just had to find private cars to take all the wounded *shabab* to the hospital," he says. There weren't enough ambulances. Nearly all wounded suffered M-16 bullets to the legs, which is where Israeli army regulations specify soldiers should direct fire at stone-throwers. "It is so emotionally exhausting," he says, doubtlessly an understatement.

We are quiet in the Mercedes from Khan Yunis to Rafah via Muraj checkpoint. In and out of this city of nearly 100,000, traffic moves by one scrutinized car at a time. We stop at the line. The young soldier scans us. I hate this. I want contact with soldiers as little as anyone else here, though I have far less to fear. He flicks his hand. Pass. I try to discuss with Mohammed our goals for today, February 8, the only afternoon until early March that Mohammed's schedule allows him time for our work. Progress is feeling uncomfortably slow after nearly a month. We aren't spending the time in Canada Camp we first envisioned, and I'm growing tense daily, as I am limited by funds to a three-month stay. Ramadan, the Muslim month of fasting, begins in two weeks. Our conversation droops. I try to envision Mohammed's morning of hauling bloodied teenagers into cars.

We drop by the house of Rowhi, now Mohammed's former supervisor from the Social Welfare Office. Back in that windowless, dry swimming pool of a living room, Mohammed brightens. Rowhi is his therapy today, as Mohammed was for

Rowhi that day after soldiers came in the night. I ask Rowhi about little Rula. She's fine, he says, thanks be to God.

My mind jumps to Canada Camp, again just 100 yards away. I try patience as they talk, but the heavy cardamom coffee rushes me with what feels like an injection and suddenly, my every anxiety is a demonic caricature that feels perfectly rational. My sympathy for Mohammed vanishes. I am obsessed with the thought that today is our one day together and we are accomplishing nothing.

But reality is kinder. Rowhi offers his house for the next two nights, my first in Tel el Sultan. In a brief visit to Hanan, she says I can photograph her at work in her school tomorrow. She is still the only woman I have met in Canada Camp.

Later, at the taxi stand, I lose my patience again. It is 6:00, nightfall, and we are late, in danger of being caught in the curfew. I desperately need to get all the way to Gaza, for a retreat to my quiet Rimal apartment before spending two nights in Canada Camp. A cab pulls up, the only one in sight. The driver tells Mohammed he'll head to Khan Yunis after he drops his passengers a few blocks away. Mohammed says we'll await his return.

As we wait, another cab pulls up, also to Khan Yunis. "Let's go," I tell Mohammed, pulling at his sleeve.

"No," he says, "we promised the other driver."

"But who knows how long he will be? Come on!"

"No. We promised him." He is firm.

Exasperated, I am about to climb into the second taxi alone when the first one returns. The driver, it turns out, is actually going all the way to Gaza. As he roars northbound, we leave the other driver shouting his destination into the dark as the curfew clock ticks down another amputated Gaza night.

Mohammed and I exchange a look and I apologize. Only later would I see our conflict clearly: Mohammed is less willing than I to subordinate relationships to productivity. After all, he is trained as a social worker and I as a journalist. Although I concede much to him, I remain unresolved. I am funded to pack home a story on Canada Camp, period. I can't imagine returning to say only, "I made a lot of good friends." I don't expect it would translate, professionally speaking.

At Rowhi's the next night, dinner comes after curfew has hung its unquiet silence about us. I sit on the floor with the family around their small, round table packed with bowls, a warm discus of bread in my hand.

From somewhere outside, a motor, another and another; a shuffling dull clomping of boots and crackling of radios and low mumblings in what must be Hebrew and each of us freezes. Hands about to gather food onto bread withdraw slowly. We listen. I soundlessly slip my camera bag under a couch out of sight and touch my passport in my shirt pocket like a talisman. The food sits. Rowhi curls two-year-old Rula into his lap with his hand. I watch her expressionless face and wonder if she understands what is going on. Not again, I hope for her sake, not this time. No window allows them to see us, or us to see them. Just the concrete wall. The house is built that way on purpose. We watch the door. More thuds and clicks and boots hurrying in sand; a shout and a reply and the motors start again. Wheels crunch the gravel and fade. Only after the silence has fully reconfigured, like ripples calming in a meddled pool, do we resume the dinner gone cold.

The next evening, I am ready to scream at my host and his four brothers. I'm exhausted from photographing Hanan's school today, and Rowhi relocated me to this house of friends in Canada Camp out of fear the soldiers might return tonight. The television blares the Egyptian channel. All four pepper me with questions in rapid Arabic slang, poking and pulling at my sleeve, commanding me to listen as if sheer volume will render the language at last comprehensible.

I slog through Arabic that feels like quicksand. Is it normal, I wonder, occasionally to become intolerably angry with your hosts? Not personally at all, but with their behavior? It's just another bout of severe culture shock, I try to counsel myself. But my timing is terrible: this is my first night in Canada Camp Palestine. Ibrahim, the eldest of my hosts, talks like a loose fire hose. At more than six-and-a-half feet, with a body strong from work at a local cinder block factory, he leans in when he talks, giving him an ominous bearing, but he's deeply supportive of what Mohammed and I are trying to do. I just find it difficult to converse with him for more than five minutes.

One of his brothers pulls out snapshots of a wedding. He parades the pictures of men and women dancing. The others carry on, relentlessly grabbing my hands, shaking my legs and tugging my sleeve. In the pictures I glimpse a family life I have yet to see in Canada Camp. As my mood plunges into depression, I wonder if I ever will. If I could speak more Arabic and understand what was happening culturally, I think, I'd be having a great time. Like them. This is a fun evening: what's my problem? The attention is just too intense. I withdraw, saying I'm tired. But I'm a fraud: I can't sleep at all after three cups of cardamom coffee, something that never happens to Gazan men.

Near noon the next day I thank Ibrahim, who spent his morning showing me the cinder block plant where he works. It's a small place. Like 90 percent of Gazan businesses, it employs less than ten people. This is due to Israeli-controlled business licensing practice: only the small businesses get the licenses. This protects Israeli firms from potential competitors in the low-wage Strip. I am profuse with my gratitude to him, hopeful that my behavior last night is forgivable, but his generosity all morning has already made it clear it is.

In a Peugeot taxi in Rafah, en route back to Gaza city and Rimal, my eyes drift shut involuntarily from exhaustion. I barely notice Muraj checkpoint approaching. But the soldier hails us into the inspection area, not straight through. I wake up at once and feel a stiffening press of adrenaline. I mentally arrange a cover story. Muraj is where ambulances en route to Nasser Hospital in Khan Yunis—there is no hospital in Rafah—

are routinely stopped following confrontations, according to UNRWA reports. Some wounded just wait and bleed here, but UNRWA also has recorded cases of wounded *shabab* being dragged from ambulances and beaten with rifles and batons.

We disembark with the quiet deliberation one adopts at gunpoint. There are six of us, total. The others form a line without being told: they know the routine. We hand our papers to one of the three soldiers, five military identity cards and a U.S. passport. Another soldier inspects the front seat, back seat, trunk, probably for weapons and, I am relieved to notice, finds none. Each ID, or *hawiyya*, is scrutinized, matched to the face, and returned. The passport is passed up to a third sentry crouched in the sandbagged booth with a mounted machine gun inside. The first soldier signals me to take one step forward out of line. The others are sent back to the taxi to wait.

"American?" he asks.

"Yes," I reply.

"Why are you here?"

I decide that acting ignorant, naive and as unhappy to be in the Strip as I presume he is might be my best defense.

"I had to do photos at one of the UNRWA schools today."

"Why?"

I shrug. "It's my job. It was arranged with UNRWA. Call them if you want." I hope he does not, because I was Hanan's guest at Rafah Elementary Girls School "D" yesterday, not today.

"I did not see you this morning." He is young, early twenties probably, with a face that would be soft if it wasn't his job to make it so hard.

"I passed in a taxi," I shrug again, lying.

"In a taxi with *them*? With Arabs?"

"Yes. Not these same men, but another taxi, yes."

"Why?" His face twists with a combination of disbelief, amazement and revulsion, telling me what has been normal for me for three weeks is nothing short of insane to him.

"It's how I was told to get here."

"By who? Who told you that?"

"At UNRWA, the PR people there."

"You know this is a closed military zone?"

"A what?" I say, genuinely thrown for a moment. I glance about. "No, uh, this is a town. A closed military zone wouldn't have people coming and going, would it? That's like a curfew, right?"

He takes a different tack at once, employing the rapid topical shifts of the professional interrogator. "Why didn't you stop and register on your way in?"

"I didn't know I had to."

"Well isn't it kind of obvious you can't just go *in there*?" He motions to the road as if he is guardian of Hades itself.

"Well, no," I reply. "There's no sign or anything. I was just told take the taxi, be friendly so it would be safe and then go to the UNRWA office in Rafah. You know there are so many rules and things here, maybe they didn't tell me—"

"And you actually took an *Arab taxi*?"

"How else do you get in and out of Rafah?"

"The bus."

"Like that?" I say, pointing to a distant, rattle-trap bus on the road.

"No!" he says, scornful now. "That's an Arab bus. There's a regular bus that comes here."

I feign interest as he recites the details. I try to imagine arriving on the outskirts of Rafah in a Jewish settler bus or, worse, asking a Gazan taxi driver to please stop for a moment while I dash over to the sentry booth to register with the soldiers for the day.

He looks at my camera bag. "You're a journalist or what?"

I am not, at the moment, a journalist; I don't want to be asked to show Israeli press credentials I don't have. Besides, I've heard many soldiers regard a foreign journalist with little more esteem than they regard an armed Palestinian. "No, I was doing pictures for a company in the States. Cultural stuff, Palestinian girls in school." I show him a genuine letter from a genuine photographic company I have carried just for this moment. As he reads, I notice the other five men sitting silently in the taxi, waiting, blank faces betraying nothing. "Look, ah, I know you have your job but is this going to take a while? I need to be back in Jerusalem this—"

The soldier in the booth speaks for the first time, the one who has been flipping pages in my passport and writing things down. "Yes, this is going to take a long time," he says, interrupting me in a tone designed to intimidate. "They in the taxi go now. You stay."

The taxi pulls away. I don't watch it.

"You know you need permission from the Civil Administration to come here." It's the first soldier again.

Closed military zone, registration and now this. "Pardon?"

"Yeah, for your own protection. It's the Wild West in there. That's how all these stone-throwing incidents start. Someone like you walks in with a camera, they see you and they start it. But they'll kill you, too, believe me they will. You're lucky you made it out alive."

"Well, I was only in the school. Nobody threw any stones. Everyone was friendly and besides, there weren't any jeeps around to throw stones at!"

"You're lucky. Really, it's the Wild West in there."

I wonder if this is an act aimed at scaring me, just as I am acting to bluff him, or if he actually does have no inkling why he is so hated "in there," or what kind of difference wearing an automatic rifle can make in how people treat you. But for the moment he is the authority, so I don't argue. I don't want this to escalate into a film confiscation: ten rolls from yesterday lie inside my bag. I ask him about this permission "if I ever have to come here again."

He explains. With it, he informs me frankly, "you can go in an IDF [Israeli Defense Forces] jeep anywhere you want and take pictures of these people, whatever you want, safely."

I stifle incredulity and keep playing along. "So why doesn't UNRWA tell me this?"

"Because UNRWA doesn't give a damn." The words tumble like rocks dumped into a gully.

I get my passport back, thank him for his advice and wait for a UN vehicle, any UN vehicle, to come along. I try to make conversation. "Must be hard working here, of all places." He doesn't take it. "We do our job," he says flatly. I don't say more. A UN van appears and, out of the soldier's earshot, I plead my predicament to the driver. The door swings open and two teachers welcome me to a seat. I feel safe again.

The next day, my head pounds from a night that belonged only to the dogs and roosters of normally somnolent Rimal. The rain is torrential today; half the sandy street below is wiped out, a small canyon carved in its place.

Long ago, in his fifteenth-century memoir, *Treatise on the Holy Land*, Father Francesco Suriano of Italy wrote, "While I was yet a layman, one winter in the city of Gaza, in 1470, owing to the great rain almost half the houses of the city collapsed." Houses may not fall down today, I think over a morning coffee, but what Mohammed calls "The Forty Days," the six-week coastal winter that just might be the origin of old Noah's forty days, has surely laid in a good siege. And Mohammed's brother Khaled's wedding is to begin tonight with the slaughter of an ox, lunch feast tomorrow.

In Gaza city, I visit my Rimal cohost Douglas at the Gaza Center for Rights and Law, the Strip's solitary and tenacious human rights agency. Douglas is their UN-funded international observer. He is tense today. His face, capable of wild grins and an articulate banter, is all business. What he tells me in run-on sentences is that the Israeli army has picked up where old Father Suriano's rain left off 500 years ago: a curfew is down on Khan Yunis, and an Israeli army jeep was ambushed in the night, two soldiers dead, probably by Hamas but nobody's sure, but worst, fieldworkers are phoning in reporting "great big goddamn explosions." An Israeli army artillery attack on forcibly vacated homes is under way. Although Israel has long dynamited the family homes of some *shabab* accused of throwing stones—a practice picked up from pre-World War II British Mandate days—these all-out attacks using battlefield artillery are a distinctive feature of Prime Minister Yitzak Rabin's 1992 Labor government. The attacks have occurred only in the Gaza Strip, and all have taken place in the vicinity of armed attacks on Israeli soldiers. This one is going on somewhere in Hope Project, *amal mashroua*, or just *amal*, as everyone calls it, a mile from Mohammed's house. I think of Khaled—what do you do if there is a curfew on your wedding day?

I phone Mohammed.

"We are fine, don't worry," he says. "But you know we are just home here, sitting, waiting so much for the news."

"What about the wedding? The ox?" I ask.

"We are just waiting. Remember, Dick, this is Gaza. When will you come?"

"As soon as the curfew is lifted, okay? What about the attack? Can you hear it?"

"So big explosions you would not believe it. I am fearing they are using the antitank missiles and heavy explosives again. If you want to photograph, many people will help you, it is so bad a one. But come soon. We are waiting for you in your home."

I hang up amazed at his gentle hospitality under fire.

The curfew endures into the night. Douglas comes back to the Rimal apartment drenched, late. Khan Yunis is a closed military zone, he reports, cracking open a can of beer that is sold in but one place in the Gaza Strip—the UN Beach Club a few blocks away. He stood at the edge of the CMZ, as he calls the closed military zone, with other legal fieldworkers—and no journalists—demanding entrance, soldiers refusing. Rumor has it a city block is gone, blown up, making this the worst of the more than a dozen such attacks since the army began them in July, 1992. The residents, Douglas says, were evacuated by the army before dawn, a few hours after the jeep was ambushed, so no people have been killed or injured. The surviving soldier from the jeep had pointed to somewhere near this block as the source of fire.

At 7:30 the next morning I walk to UNRWA's Gaza compound.

"No more curfew, go!" says one of the watchmen.

The road is clear and the rain has stopped. The hangdog streets of Khan Yunis don't betray what's on everyone's mind. Next door to Mohammed's, boys arrange wicker stools under a carport. The wedding is on. Ibtisam tells me Mohammed is at the butcher's, struggling to get the ox cooked by afternoon. "Come back by two!" she calls as I walk out to find a taxi to *amal*, to Hope.

To the first driver I say, "Amal?"

"Get in, let's go!" he says as if helping a foreigner with a camera is today a matter of patriotic duty.

Amal mashroua looks a lot like Canada Camp Palestine, only larger and older. It was part of the same Israeli development scheme of the late 1970s and early 1980s that resulted in Tel el Sultan. Extended families received small plots upon which they built tall houses, mostly two to five stories with louvered windows on the upper floors and tall metal doors for shops at street level. Only a few are painted. Near where Amal is separated from a hundred yards of pure sand and the Gush Qatif Jewish settlement, near a line of trash piled like plowed snow, the driver stops. To the right, he says, is Block 52. Or was.

Block 52 has become a grim spectacle. Hundreds of men and boys stand about as if this was a citywide rite of visitation, a gathering in crisis not unlike that offered the man shot in Rafah ten days ago. I greet the first man I pass and verify directions to make social contact and feel at ease under the heavy gazes.

At the first house, I am ushered like a diplomat to where men bucket-brigade salvaged possessions through a six-foot hole in what was a kitchen. Plates. An electric fan. Two coffee pots. All covered with dust and ash and soot. I clamber over piles of bricks and broken lumber, saying "Peace be upon you" and nodding amidst the crowd, photographing intensely, shooing away boys angrily in Arabic, the way I imagine any of the other men might, boys who even today try to jump in front of my camera, smiling and chanting "How are you!" I am introduced to Adel Tanira amidst rubble. We shake hands gravely. Nine people in his family, he tells me in a voice that sounds beaten. All homeless now. "And all of our money and jewelry from the bedroom is gone, too," he adds.

I look about at the young boys gathered. What, I wonder, will *amal*, the everyday word for "hope," mean to them now? A Palestinian UN worker appoints himself my escort and I am grateful. Most of the block is eerily quiet, in a state of collective shock. The destruction has transformed the home from the most private of places to the most public. All complex codes of courtesy are waived today. No offers of tea or coffee. No kitchens. We walk in, shake hands, take pictures, take notes, and leave, living rooms, bedrooms, kitchens and bathrooms, whole walls gone, reinforced concrete slab ceilings hanging by twisted steel rods, cracked, roofs open to sky, possessions strewn and crushed and burnt, orderly homes of families as ordinary as the one next door blasted into ten thousand sharp and broken pieces scattered on the ground. Sharp shards everywhere; walking is treacherous. In rooms still intact, women sort clothes pulled from wedding wardrobes sprayed with automatic gunfire; they point out bullet holes in mirrors, ceilings, pillows and even an exploded porcelain toilet. More women complain about missing their gold jewelry, the traditional form of women's wealth given as dowry in marriage; men say what Adel Tanira said, too: bundles of dollars and Jordanian dinars, personal savings in a society denied banks, are gone, too, looted or burned by vengeful soldiers. One woman watches me walk in the front door of her house, cringes briefly, and commences a tearful grieving. I hesitate. Do I frighten her? Am I a vision of an enemy, of an imperial power that always leaves photographers in the wake of its soldiers? Her young daughter clings to her dress and, seeing her mother weeping, begins the same. Men stand about impassively, nodding at me to photograph them. I fulfill my duty, attending with care to technical demands of the photographic act—lens choice and focus and exposure and composition—keeping my shutter speed high because my hands are shaking.

In the street, a Gazan fieldworker from the Gaza Center for Rights and Law tells me he counts ten houses beyond repair;

nine others salvageable; and 186 people homeless. His recitation of international law is practiced: this is collective punishment, a "grave breach" of Article 33 of the 1949 Fourth Geneva Convention, he tells me, which Israel signed but has since 1967 refused to recognize as applicable to the West Bank and Gaza Strip. Such "grave breaches," he makes sure I note, are actual war crimes punishable by international prosecution. I walk away imagining the international reaction if an armed Palestinian faction blew up nineteen Israeli homes following an ambush on two Palestinian guerrillas.

"Excuse me, please," a bearded man in a wool overcoat stops me and says in good English. "Excuse me, that was my house, that one. They can take all of our houses. They already took our land. They can blow up our homes again and again. So what? We can build them again. It only makes us the stronger ones. Tell that, excuse me, where are you from?"

"United States. I'm a journalist."

"Tell that to America," he continues with the modulated passion of the well-educated. "To Mr. Bush and Mr. Clinton. They can destroy our houses, but this makes us come together."

Later I gather details of how the residents of Block 52 spent the day the explosions ripped the air. Women and children were herded into several nearby houses and searched by two female soldiers. Men were blindfolded and handcuffed in a nearby school, interrogated one by one but not beaten. Two were arrested for charges unrelated to the ambush. Soldiers searched each house in Block 52 for hidden "wanted men," activists known to the occupation authorities, even employing a dog. No wanted men were found. Then, instead of leaving, the army fired antitank missiles and 40mm shells at the homes, planted TNT in living rooms and bombed still more with TNT from a helicopter. All day long, everyone knew exactly what was happening.

In the last house, I spot Ahmed, whom I had last seen at Omar's wedding. His face is heavier than usual, his jaw unmoving, his beard as nascent as a few days ago. We greet

After a morning spent combing the ashes of her family bedroom for her jewelry, this woman told me she found only a few items and presumed the rest—mostly her gold bracelets—to have been looted by soldiers before they set off a dynamite charge in the room.

warmly despite the circumstance. "This house on the corner, this house belongs to my aunt," he says without emotion. There is no roof anywhere; every room has been shattered with explosives. We wander the wreckage together, silently. He seems calm, but this, Mohammed has told me, is the time of *sargat el sikineh*, an Arabic idiom meaning "knife shock," the first moments after a deep wound wherein the body is paralyzed but the pain has yet to fully set in. Psychologically, it is the time of disorientation that precedes real grieving, depression and rage, all necessary steps in coping with such victimization. It is a feeling, he has said, with which Gazans are all too well acquainted.

"What will they do?" I finally ask Ahmed.

He shrugs. "They will stay with some of our relatives. Others will get tents." He pulls me outside to point out a Catholic Relief Services van already unloading blankets.

By early afternoon, he and I thread our way through the maze of camp passageways, "the snakeways," for the mile from Amal to Mohammed's house and Khaled's wedding feast. Walking with Ahmed here I feel great security. This is his turf.

The carport is packed. I barely get to say hello to a beaming Mohammed whose attention is leaping from one man to the next, greeting each of the dozens streaming through the camp alley with handshakes, cheek kisses and his easy laugh. He tells me how he and his brothers snuck out last night during curfew to slaughter the ox.

I listen, incredulous. "But Mohammed," I say, "how did you know there would be no curfew this morning? How did you know the curfew wouldn't be extended?"

"Most times with these house demolition operations now it is this way. The next day there is no curfew because they know people will be so angry, and so they leave. Today I assure you will not see a soldier anywhere near Khan Yunis." He grins. "So you see it is so nice here now. You do everything the family does—this is your home, okay?"

Lunch is precisely the same menu served at Omar's feast last week: heaps of saffron rice, hunks of beef and bottles of cola and 7-Up. Serving takes the same frantic style, too, as *shabab* pass platter after platter, each boy taking pride in his speed and agility of delivery.

It's after dark when Khaled, the groom, finally sits down inside the house with Suzanne, the bride. Though arranged, the union is, Khaled assured me earlier, one of mutual consent and even enthusiasm. They face their families, women on one side, men on the other. For a short while there are songs and clapping in the impossibly crowded room, but, Mohammed tells me, "it is nothing like what would be a real celebration," where drums and flutes and tambourines would lead dancing into the night. Tonight is subdued, he says, "out of respect for the families in Amal." For five years of *intifada*, wedding celebrations were canceled altogether lest they affront the hundreds of families grieving death and injury and imprisonment. The ban was lifted last summer. Tonight, quiet but not canceled, is a compromise.

Khaled and Suzanne both ask me to take pictures of them. His suit is new, stiff and green with sharp lapels; his hair is perfectly trimmed and his posture straight. Her dress is iridescent. It billows with lace and froths with puffy frills. Her eyes are nearly masked with kohl, and her cheeks are tinted dark with rouge. They sit together on a small bench under a black-velvet tapestry of the Ka'ba in Mecca, the holiest site in Islam, specially nailed to the cinder block wall. They look at me: proud, self-conscious in the spotlight of attention, profoundly nervous, smiling, a bit forced and a bit sincere, as best they can, under the circumstances.

Amal.

Hanging out after school: Upon high school graduation, Canada Camp Egypt youth are barred from attending college in the Gaza Strip or West Bank. The few who can afford Egyptian universities must pay the higher tuitions charged foreign students.

CHAPTER 6
CANADA CAMP, EGYPT

L ike the U.S.-Mexico border described by Alan
Riding in his book *Distant Neighbors*, passage to
Rafah, Egypt, is very much "from organization to improvisa-
tion." Israel's terminal, built around the time of the 1982
withdrawal from Sinai, is trim, white stucco with a watered
lawn. In the air-conditioned hall, foreigners and Israelis line
up for one pair of computer-keying immigration officials
while Palestinians from the occupied territories line up for
another, separate pair. A shuttle bus plies the 100 yards
beyond a gate, through layers of fencing and over a trench into
Egypt's North Sinai province, where, in a hot, low metal
building like a warehouse, platoons of more officials clatter
out travel records on manual typewriters, and the air itself
tastes stained by black tea and Cleopatra cigarettes.

I'm alone. For Mohammed to receive a visa to Egypt, he
would have spent what usually amounts to days sitting, waiting
for an intimidatingly detailed interrogation with Shin Bet, Israel's
domestic intelligence. There was never a doubt I would have to
visit Canada Camp, Egypt, without him. Now, it's just as well.
My battered taxi from the border is piloted by an unabashed
Egyptian informer, a self-described "government driver," into
whose Citroen I was escorted the moment I announced
mukhayim kanada as my destination outside the border station.
Mohammed would not be enjoying this. I'm not either.

At an unmarked, windowless, intelligence office, disturbingly far from the main road, I explain I am joining the
UNRWA rations distribution team in their bimonthly ritual
upon which four out of five Canada Camp residents depend.
"I have UN permission," I assure the sunglassed man holding
my passport. "Okay," he says, adding a theatrical smile, "Have

a nice time in Egypt. Welcome."

North from town, along the road to the coast, a dirt track points right a few hundred yards through scattered homes and an orchard to Canada Camp. We bump right again at the sign in misspelled English, "Wellcome to Canada Camp / Cleanliness is Next to Godliness," all the way up Middle Street, the half-mile-long, sewage-puddled, alley-wide, unpaved main thoroughfare and halt at the blue gate of the Khadija Bint Khoweilid school, the camp's lone educational institution. It's dusk already.

"Dick!" I hear shouted from a figure in a gray *jalabeeya*. The man approaches across the sand, arms wide. Not until we are face to face do I recognize Khalil Audeh, UNRWA's ration supervisor from Gaza city, whom I have met before only in a suit and tie. His old eyes glimmer in delight at my confusion. "Welcome to 'Hilton Canada,'" he says, leading me with mock formality to a classroom where a half dozen men sit on a rough, gray blanket surrounded by piles of foam mattresses, cardboard boxes and more blankets. A hissing propane camp stove warms tea. Ten of us will sleep here, he explains as I remove my shoes and shake hands with the men, all Gazans. They, like Khalil, have come from across the border to work the distribution. Khalil offers bread and goat cheese carved with a pocketknife, my first food since breakfast. "I feel so happy here," he tells me. "What is Canada Camp? It is so poor, but there are no clashes, no curfews, no occupation. Life seems more relaxed. For us"—he sweeps his hand to include the others—"it is like a holiday."

"But Khalil, Egyptian security seems tighter in some ways than Israeli occupation!" I say, remembering the intelligence office a few minutes ago, the repatriates who say they speak more freely in occupied Palestine, and the stories of the seventy or more Canada Camp *shabab* deported from Egypt to Libya, stories to which I have yet to be able to attach details.

"I know," he replies. "But you don't know what it is like just to get away from *them* for a few days, to know you can walk with no curfew, without seeing the soldiers."

In another classroom, Abu Hassan is supervising remodeling. He greets me coolly, preoccupied it seems by the questions of the carpenters. As camp director, Mohammed Al Najjar, or Abu Hassan, as everyone calls him, is a foreigner visitor's liaison with the formidable bureaucracies of Egypt and UNRWA. He keeps his hands in the pockets of his belted trench coat. A thin sweep of gray hair tops his impassive, sculptured face. He weights words with silences. My access to the camp is entirely in his hands.

Last time Abu Hassan saw me I was on my way to Gaza a month ago. I could not walk about and photograph in Canada Camp Egypt, he had explained, without government clearance. The longest he could obtain permission for me to stay would be three days.

"You must understand my position," he had said. "I am made responsible for everything that goes on in the camp. The authorities are very clear with me. If there is to be a foreign visitor, I must make him known to them. They are very, well, nervous. If I was not to tell them, then, well." He tossed his hands into the air and smiled. "Without the permission, I can do nothing. You can do nothing."

I sensed frustration had long ago metamorphosed, under geological layers of politics, into compromise and a clear sense of a proscribed radius of authority. "If you come with the *tamween* [the bimonthly UN ration distribution team], you will be most welcome. This is the best. It is the only way to stay overnight." Three days in February; three more in April: that would be all, provided I could clear my permission in Gaza.

Now, he tells me to come to his office in the morning to discuss my permission to photograph.

Back in "Hilton Canada," smoke stings my eyes, murky as a tavern. Men sit about the gray blanket under rows of fluorescent lights. Talk flies loud and fast about two subjects: politics and prices. Most goods in Egypt cost half or less what they do in Gaza. Shortly, an old man limps my way, squinting and blinking myopically behind bottle-glass spectacles. He must be from the camp; he is too old to be a worker from Gaza. He leans close to what he ascertains is the vicinity of my face. I try not to flinch. I only get this close to someone I'm about to kiss.

"F-f-fuck . . . *Am-reeka*!!" he explodes, stuttering at a madman's volume, "f-fuck shit *Amreeka*!" And in Arabic, "What do we ever get from America but shit!! Shit!! Shit!! Shit!!"

Khalil jumps up and pulls him back, shouts down his raving, and they argue as I wipe my face with my sleeve.

"I am so sorry," says Khalil. "I was just telling our good friend Abu Khaled you are our guest and not Mr. Clinton. Please forgive us."

After a moment of shock, I find the breach of decorum refreshing. "No, Khalil," I say. "Crude, maybe, but he is more honest than insulting. Maybe many people in Gaza would like to say this same thing but they don't because I am a guest?" I turn to Abu Khaled and assure him I won't take it personally. He smirks wickedly and retreats; a bit loony, actually, I think.

Khalil nods gravely. "Unfortunately you are probably right," he says. "There is no justice, Dick. I have seen the British and the Israelis and the Americans. They still treat us as if we were not human, us Palestinians." He shifts the subject to his upcoming retirement after a forty-year career with UNRWA.

Somewhere around six in the morning, I waken to the sharp smell of cigarettes newly lit. Khalil is up already; he carries a demitasse of cardamom coffee to my mat with grandfatherly solicitude, eyes wide like Christmas morning. "It's going to be great," he says. "We'll start passing out rations in a few hours!" His enthusiasm is contagious; I wonder how he'd look in a Santa Claus suit. Too thin; his cigarettes would burn the beard.

Abu Hassan is kind this morning and apologizes for his distraction last night. An office assistant brings us tea. In the small, square, well-organized office at the corner of the school compound, Abu Hassan requests a list of all I want to photograph—for the *mukhabarat*, of course. He reminds me that photographing the border, or any people shouting to relatives at The Calling Wall, would result in my ejection from the camp and, possibly, revocation of my visa. The permission will take a few hours; until then I can walk and photograph only within the school. "That is UNRWA's jurisdiction," he explains. "The rest of the camp is Egypt."

The Khadija Bint Khoweilid school is the only civic institution in Canada Camp, except for perhaps the UNRWA clinic with its doctor and two nurses. Built in 1972, it was intended only as an elementary school for the camp of just more than 4,000. Now, its fourteen classrooms serve all levels of students from a slightly larger population in three shifts: middle school in the morning, elementary in the afternoon and secondary in the evening. A tiny office for two UNRWA social workers is here at the school, too; so is the shed now piled with burlap sacks and boxes for the rations; so are two rooms for women's vocational classes in hairdressing and sewing; and so is the slightly warped ping-pong table, the only recreational facility in Canada Camp other than the dirt soccer field next to one of the two mosques. There is no library here. No clubs. No after-school activities. No movies. Not a cafe in all the camp.

In the school yard, which is all sand, stray middle school pupils wander and a dozen men stack 110-pound bags of sugar, rice and flour almost to the ceiling of the *tamween* shed. The men, camp residents, have been hired to labor under the Gazan crew for three days at twenty Egyptian pounds, or about six dollars, a day. As I approach, several of the young ones drop their tasks, begin shouting and surround me, grabbing my jacket and vying for position, mocking muscle-man poster boys, loudly demanding pictures, all without so much as a handshake or a "Peace be upon you." I feel like a goaded monkey. The pictures might be funny, I think, but I hate feeling manipulated. Conversation proves futile. I select the final, embarrassing option of retreat. When I emerge from the "Hilton" after a few minutes, Ahmed, the dour and rotund young security guard, calls me away for tea, preventively no doubt, and I cannot refuse.

The *tamween* begins at noon. It's first come first serve, but there is always, Abu Hassan assures me, enough to go around. Of the camp's 4,400 residents, 3,350 are on the rolls for this two-month period. Representatives of families gather at the gate clutching bags and buckets and plastic jugs. Names are checked on the list, typewritten in English, and a red card handed to each representative with quantities due filled in. The line moves from rice to bulgur wheat to sugar to flour. At the corner of the shed, fifty-five-gallon drums of cooking oil are tapped like wine casks. Dried milk comes next, followed by tinned meat, tomatoes, and infant cereals. Most families spend an Egyptian pound, about thirty cents, to hire a two-wheel donkey cart for home delivery. It will take two full days to pass out all the food: Khalil knows this, he says, because this is the sixty-fourth bimonthly distribution since April 25, 1982, the day of the border.

The *tamween* is as close to a carnival as comes to Canada Camp Egypt. Boys fill the yard when classes recess, and each time I raise my camera the hooting begins. I don't photograph much and hope that in a while I'll cease to be a novelty. Women and men cluster here and there. The donkey cart drivers help families load up. Old Abu Khaled, who had announced his opinion of the U.S. government with such passion last night, totters about on his cane, hollering greetings to friends he can barely see. I realize he must be nearly deaf, too. It is mid-afternoon when Abu Hassan approaches to tell me intelligence has granted my permission to go where I please, except, he reminds me, "don't go near the border."

The grid streets of Canada Camp are solidly lined with the low, uneven, contiguous concrete-block houses of other Gaza Strip refugee camps, with only one difference: Palestinian flags have always been permitted display here. Flags appear on doors, walls, car bumpers, and I spot a man in a flag-motif jacket. Everything, it seems, is red, green, black or white. In one section of the camp, however, several dozen houses lie bulldozed into rubble. I shiver slightly, remembering *amal mashroua* in Khan Yunis, but this is Block One, Canada Camp, a ghost town now. This is where Hanan, Mustafa, Hazim and all the others now in Tel el Sultan lived. Abu Hassan noted forty-four Egyptian families have been assigned by their government to the best Block One homes left standing after other camp residents pillaged the abandoned homes for building materials. Relations among these families and the camp are "complex," he said, implying a diplomatic euphemism.

A half dozen men hail me into a small grocery. The owner is stocking shelves that line the perimeter of the room. A bottle of orange soda appears in my hand. The rituals of such conversations are familiar by now, and they interview me far more than I interview them:

America.

Married.

No children, but soon, God willing.

Journalist.

Occupation must end because "the land is Palestine." Here I keep just which land I am referring to deliberately vague—the presently occupied territories or those plus the state of Israel—to accommodate the possibility of several political viewpoints.

They ask about their former neighbors now in Tel el Sultan. Faces hang soberly as I detail the complaints I've heard about the cost of living, unemployment and the multifaceted, ubiquitous occupation. Then I wonder: is what I'm describing worse than idleness under the scrutiny of Egypt? Am I soiling the healthy romanticism of exiles for the homeland, sullying dreams before their time? Desperation is thick in eyes and words. "Every day I just want to wake up in Palestine," says one, leaving my caveats ignored, "every day, every day."

Late that night, the "Hilton" is teeming with visitors, as rowdy as a post-game locker room. The propane stove whistles up pot after pot of tea. The man next to my bunk snores phlegmatically through it all. After a full day of grappling with Arabic, I withdraw quietly. We all share a snack of bread, sharp cheese and *zaatar*, a popular, thyme-based spice. I melt into the warm camaraderie in which I nonetheless sense a manic, even destructive edge, an unintended seepage of pressurized rage.

After no more than two hours sleep, the 4:30 A.M. prayer call is heeded en masse. My eyes sting from smoke. Breakfast is more bread, cheese and *zaatar*. Ration distribution is at 6:30; I set out into the camp.

From what feels like a permissible distance, I stand in the street and gaze at the border. No one is at the wall, The Calling Wall, at this hour. The no-man's-land is dotted up and down with watchtowers where figures stand silhouetted in the clear morning, like gargoyles.

Raji, who tells me he is a carpenter, spots me in the street and calls me over to a plastic mat outside his home and shop. It's a kind of a porch with corrugated metal walls on two sides. His face is blotchy, drawn and unshaven. Despite his portly belly, I wonder about his nutrition. When I tell him I have visited Tel el Sultan, he tells me his name is on the 1992 repatriation list, among the thirty-five families waiting to move to Tel el Sultan since September. Their sole impediment has been the lack of their $12,000 construction assistance checks, provided through 1992 by a now-broke PLO via Egyptian banks. No one has yet offered to replace the PLO as donor.

"We were promised the money would come 'this week, or maybe next week,' for months now," he says in English. "This is what we get told. So for the last six months I just sleep. I can't get work—who wants to give me work if I may leave tomorrow?"

He shows me his workshop, dark and idle. Band saw, two table saws, benches, piles of scrap wood, a neat rack of tools. "Business used to be okay," he shrugs. Now, he's converted the front room of his house into a tiny store with sparse displays of candy and toiletries. This, he tells me, brings in about a dollar a day, but he needs at least three dollars a day to feed two wives, six children, his mother, a brother and two sisters.

He offers tea and a tray of homemade, jam-filled short-bread squares doused in powdered sugar. I instruct his son Mohammed, who looks about four, to go inside and tell his mother right away thank you, it is delicious. Raji complains again about "the situation," and then changes the subject. "Sometimes all we ever talk about here is politics," he says. "It gets boring. Tell me about America, what is your life like there?"

By mid-morning the sun is bright, even warm. On another street, a man approaches and asks if I can help him pen a letter in English. He wants to apply to UNRWA for a job, he explains. "Yusef," he replies when I consent to his request and introduce myself by name. Quickly a crowd of nearly twenty packs the closet-sized shop full of glassware we have ducked into. He is to repatriate in 1994, he explains, and the best jobs in the Gaza Strip are with UNRWA. He trained in Cairo as a nurse, and he wants to apply early. But in this group there are bitter, snide remarks at the mention of UNRWA. Heads shake. I ask why.

"Because we are Barberi," Yusef says.

"What do you mean?"

"We are all from Barbera, a village near Isdud, from before '48. Israel destroyed it."

"I still don't understand," I say, holding out my hands.

"All the UNRWA jobs here go to people from Isdud. There are maybe fifty who work for UNRWA in Canada Camp. All *isdudi*, all of them. Except a few from Barbera. And we are maybe 20 percent of Canada Camp!"

I tell him about my conversation with old Abu Yasser in Tel el Sultan, who said UNRWA workers are resented and called "the dollar people" by Canada Camp have-nots.

"Yes, yes," everyone seems to throw out at once. With the letter finished, I excuse myself by announcing I must visit the UNRWA health clinic, even if it is, I add, an *isdudi* place.

Several older teenage boys escort me. After they have asked me questions, I ask, "Can you talk with girls in school?"

"Well, we see them of course," replies one, "and we all

know who we like and who we don't like. But if someone sees you talking to one of the girls, this is forbidden, very, very forbidden." He waves his finger in front of his face and tisks.

"So you never talk to them? Not even secretly?" I say, prodding perhaps beyond the bounds of civility, but I hope not.

"No. We can't." He is firm. "The camp is, as you see, very crowded. Sometimes you can look at a girl, and maybe she sees you, but that's all, and even then, that is forbidden, too."

The health clinic, on the opposite side of the camp from the school, is marked by a diminutive blue sign—all UNRWA facilities use the same shade of blue—and several tires that mark out a parking space for whenever a car shows up. There is one today, and a nice one at that.

Inside the atrium surrounded on two sides by a half dozen small examining rooms, I am introduced to Dr. Ayyoub Al Alim, chief of UNRWA health programs for Gaza Strip, who is, by coincidence, visiting today. His suit is impeccable; he has the gravitas of a statesman. I ask him if, medically speaking, Canada Camp differs from other Gaza Strip camps.

"We see more mental health problems here," he replies. "More psychosomatic diseases, particularly among young mothers and adolescents. Especially girls."

I ask him to elaborate.

"Stress, depression you know. People are too confined. It makes them crazy. Men can go out of the house, out of the camp. But the women stay in the home, and have to live in an overcrowded house, usually with several families in space designed for one."

In a few minutes Dr. Nazmi Awad, the camp doctor, steps into the atrium for a cigarette break. He is a short, intense man with thick, black-framed glasses. Patient visits, he says, average six minutes. Anyone requiring more than a basic prescription or injection must go to El Arish, an hour west. The closest hospital is in Cairo. I ask him about depression.

"I am lucky," he says, "because like the few teachers, I have work here that feels meaningful. Maybe three-fourths of the men have no work at all. So I see about one psychosomatic case a day. But I also see hypertension from stress, from not having enough money, from being separated from families across the border. There are about twenty cases of severe, chronic depression we treat with drugs. What else can you expect? We are just here waiting. Years. Oh, and scabies. We see a lot of that in the children. From the lack of money, mostly."

Walking back to the school it is late afternoon. A tall man in a new, green LaCoste polo shirt stops me.

"What are you doing here?" he asks sternly. "Why this camp? The things that affect our life are not things you can see here. And by the way, my name is Atif Nasser. I am a teacher with UNRWA."

I introduce myself, and explain my desire to document daily life in the camp and Tel el Sultan.

"I don't think that the differences between the life here and the life there are so important," he says in a tone he might use for a delinquent pupil. "Why don't you tell people about our problem with Israel? This is the important thing, the root problem. We are only a symptom of this. We are not so important. We are pawns."

He says he must go. He shakes my hand; I feel dismissed. And disoriented. He's right, of course, in a way.

By departure I am ill with a thumping headache. A third night of industrial-strength smoke and little sleep—thanks to much too much coffee and tea yesterday, at least one obligatory glass per visit—and I am staggering like a crash survivor. The *tamween* shed is empty now, the donkey drivers gone until April. I join Khalil and four others in a Cairo-bound, charter jitney piloted by one of the several dozen camp residents who garner a day or two of work a month as drivers on the Cairo-Rafah road. My companions get three vacation days in Cairo. I plan on the same. I need a break.

I am unblinking as Rafah town drifts by. The Bank of Alexandria with its polished brass sign, the rows of metal doors opening to shops for hardware, groceries, machine repair and sandwiches: it's too brief a passing, a tired testimony to the economically peripheral status of Rafah up in the forgotten far northeast of the country. In front of multistory, bureaucratic-looking buildings, a trio of men stand in the road, each wearing a navy blue *jalabeeya* and a spotless white turban, like natty Bedouin. They stop us. How ironic, I think—a checkpoint.

The men speak to our driver, and we turn down a side street. We stop at a grimy derelict built in an architectural style best described as provincial penitentiary. Men appear, their faces in keeping with the architecture, only one in uniform: *mukhabarat*, State Security Investigation, minions of what is one of the world's more formidable government intelligence networks. They unload the top rack and trunk, unzipping and untying and poking. At a box containing six one-quart, plastic bags of dried milk and twelve one-pound tins of dried meat, they stop and point. An argument begins. The minions, I sense, are up to no good. I keep my camera conspicuous as the only deterrent to violence I have. My head is throbbing. Thoughts of a shower 350 miles away in Cairo only make it worse.

"Your passport please," says one agent in English. I comply, and ask what is the problem.

"These men are smuggling. They are under arrest."

"What are they smuggling?" I ask.

"This," he says sharply, pointing at the contested box, "is stolen from the United Nations."

Khalil shuttles back and forth from the car to a filthy, dim room where a single official sits, more dungeon than office. "I have papers showing this stuff came from Gaza," he says, "but they won't accept them. These are gifts one of the men brought and we registered them." Then, "I am so sorry, Dick, I know you want to get to Cairo."

Dear Khalil, I think, about to be arrested by pirates and he apologizes for inconveniencing his guest.

"Khalil, what can I do?" I ask, holding his hand.

"Don't worry. We have called Abu Hassan and the chief of the customs office. But it will take some time."

One of the less well-dressed minions signals me to get back into the car. He and I must go to the border terminal, he says.

"Why? I have my visa and I have permission to be here from the *mukhabarat*."

"Someone wants to talk to you," he says in a heavy voice lifted out of a gangster movie and translated to Arabic.

"Who?"

"The uncle."

I raise my eyebrows and watch for a betrayal of what surely must be humor. None. Indeed. We are silent in the car.

At the terminal we wade through tourists on the daily Cairo-Tel Aviv bus caravan. He takes my arm, as if I might bolt.

I am presented to the commanding officer of intelligence. A subordinate hands my escort a ten-pound note and dismisses him.

The commanding officer—"the uncle," I presume—is a disgruntled, fidgety man who stares at his desk while his plain-clothes translator does the questioning. The translator is civil and brief. What did I do in Canada Camp? Who did I talk to? I stay vague and polite. An hour later, I'm back at the chewed-up-spit-out building in Rafah. More officials here now.

"They do this because they know we are weak," says Khalil, whose normally wide brown eyes have gone narrow. "Really, I prefer the Israelis to these men. The Israelis have a law, even though it's a bad one. They are more predictable."

"So are they still arresting everyone?"

"They are saying this."

The English-speaking agent spots me and informs me I can no longer stay with the group. I must find another taxi to Cairo at once, he says. So you want no witnesses, I think, and keep the thought to myself. I tell him I insist on staying. Impossible. I write out a phone number in Cairo, where I plan to spend my three days' break from Gaza, and press it into Khalil's hand. "Call me if I can help in any way, okay?"

The thought of Khalil spending just one night of his precious Cairo holiday in jail infuriates me, but I am powerless. Kind of like being Palestinian, I think for a moment. Kind of.

The Cairo road is a lullaby, a thread of meditation winding four hours among dunes, connecting scraggly Bedouin villages where white flags herald from rooftops the eligibility of daughters for marriage. Camels gaze from a giant horizon, laconic, chewing methodically. Solitary specks of black-wrapped Bedouin women herd distant goats. Rusty tank turrets float half-submerged in the sands where Egypt lost 27,000 of its sons in two wars since 1967, wars that cost Israel less than one-tenth as many of its own. On the way I count checkpoints. Four in Sinai, and two more across the oily blue stripe of the Suez Canal, along the four-lane highway where traffic builds and tension breaks and then every car is run like an aging thoroughbred into the honking anonymous din of Cairo.

I head for a suburb where lacy trees line a canyon of apartment blocks. Here no curfew restrains the city's pulsing night. Here men and women converse freely again. Here the discourse of military occupation, oppression and liberation feels again distanced and abstracted, just like it does back home, and I breathe a sigh of relief. But in my next breath, I wonder how Mohammed's family is on this day, and I know at that moment just how fond of them I have grown.

Khalil never calls.

CHAPTER 7
RAMADAN

From minarets, watchers of the skies carried news to the Muslim world last night: the new moon gave way to the first brilliant trace of its waxing crescent. The ninth month of our year, 1,414 years since Prophet Mohammed made his epochal flight from Mecca to Medina, has begun. Amidst the sullen decrepitude of the Egyptian border terminal, a tinselly garland tacked to a wall spells "*ramadan mabruk*," "blessed Ramadan." In the Mercedes taxi from the border to Gaza city, it seems odd that no one smokes and no food passes among us, but such is Ramadan. The mood is upbeat. And after three days in Cairo, so am I.

Ramadan is about purification. For the next twenty-eight days there will be no food, drink, smoking, sex or unkind words from sunrise to sundown. As if to offset this deprivation, feasting and visiting is encouraged in the evening, making Ramadan the favorite month of the year for many. In the Gaza Strip, the hated night curfew has cut every Ramadan party short for five years. Among the young, angry and religious, the ideal of purification is often taken to also mean the liberation of stolen land. Furthermore, it is well known that the Muslim who falls fighting for honor or land while fasting achieves the highest of martyrs' ranks. Mohammed's explanation of this had been a warning: expect confrontations during Ramadan.

But today, nothing could feel more distant or implausible. Groves of low almond trees sprout frostings of delicate white flowers. In wide fields, men heft basketball-sized cabbages onto horse-drawn carts. The air fairly tingles. I crank down the window and breathe for the sheer pleasure of it. The army checkpoints at Muraj, Kfar Darom and Netzarim are open. Occupation weighs lightly on this late February day, as if to

Evening prayers at home in Tel el Sultan. Not many men, I observed, pray fully five times a day in strict accordance with the directive set forth in the Qur'an. However, many—if not most—observe the ten-minute prayer each evening at sunset, called maghrib.

tease at some unreal, bygone era. But it is only coincidence
this day comes with Ramadan. The Islamic calendar is lunar
rather than solar, and thus Islamic dates shift ahead ten days
relative to each year's seasons.

Rimal is silent. Ramadan days are also listless times I've
heard, hours waiting only for the westward slip of sun. I
unpack and call UNRWA for news about Khalil Audeh and
his *mukhabarat* troubles. Only a night attendant answers.
Sorry, he says, the office closes an hour early in Ramadan.

At Mohammed's house in Khan Yunis Camp, I walk through
the corrugated-metal pantry through the back door into a
party. An enormous *iftar*, the fast-breaking dinner, is under way
on the floor of the small television room: piles of tiny fried fish,
rice, tomato sauce, hummus, cheese and fresh orange juice.

Mohammed rises to greet me, beaming, announcing,
"Tonight we have three celebrations: one is Ramadan, two is
your safe return from Egypt, and three—I have today received
the news about my scholarship in Britain." Of several dozen
overseas scholarships offered to Palestinians of the West Bank
and Gaza Strip, the handful of British Council advanced
degree awards are among the most prized. He'll start the one-
year program in September, he says, directing me to the mat
where four-year-old Sherif is poised to drape a sloppy hug
around my neck. Ibtisam and the kids will stay behind, he
adds. I tighten my face in concern.

"You know this is our experience as a people," he replies,
dimming his enthusiasm into pragmatism. "Many men must
leave their families for some time, to get work or training. It is
our life here. It is not our choice, but it is the only way now to
get a good education. Certainly there is nothing in Gaza."

I spot Suzanne across the circle of the family, now married
eleven days to Khaled. She attends more scrupulously to the
small children and to the bowls of food than she does to feed-
ing herself. Now it is she, not I, who is the latest newcomer to
the family. She looks neither happy nor sad. I cannot know or
even imagine her thoughts; the high wall of custom blocks a
conversation I would, under other circumstances, initiate.

"Are you going to fast?" calls Ahmed who, at eight, will begin his fasting in earnest next year.

"*Insha'allah,*" I say, not having really thought about it.

"No, please," Mohammed turns to me firmly, "I do not advise you to try this. It will be more difficult for you because it is not your tradition. You will be more tired than us. And for us, it is no problem to see someone who is not Muslim eating in Ramadan. Some even say it is good, because it makes the discipline of the Muslims stronger."

This takes me by surprise. "You mean it's not insulting for non-Muslims to eat in front of Muslims in Ramadan?"

"Not here in this house! And not in Gaza Strip. Maybe in some other countries, yes. But here, eat as you please. On the streets though, no, don't eat there, some might get angry," he qualifies. "But here in your home is okay."

"But when I am here or in Canada Camp," I protest, "I want to see and feel the same life as everyone else."

"Okay, but you will see it is not easy."

It is nearly 7:00. Mohammed's brother-in-law drops by. For Ramadan, the Israeli authorities have let out the nocturnal leash by two hourly notches. Curfew stands at 9:00 now. "They do this to prevent violence," says Mohammed. "The hours after Ramadan dinners are the most enjoyable and social time of the whole year. In other countries, visiting and parties can go on all night. But here in Gaza Strip we only get a few hours."

Sometime in the middle of the night I'm wakened by an insistent, blaring brightness. Fluorescent tubes, all stuttering and then shouting greenish light at once. Mohammed had warned me about this, too. Luckily all I have to do is slither over to the plastic sheet, still wrapped in my bedding blankets. The others stagger in slowly: Rateb with slippers over his heavy socks; Aysha with baby Abed wrapped in a blanket; Mohammed barefoot on the concrete floor. Ten-year-old Suha has the worst time: even as she tears off bites of bread her eyes drift shut. The clock reads 4:10 A.M.

Mohammed's mother has hard-boiled the eggs, sliced the cheese, scooped out the jam and warmed the beans and bread for the day's *suhur*, the meal before sunrise. The women, I am told, rotate this assignment. We eat in bleary silence. Occasionally someone says something monosyllabic. Mohammed fires up his first and last cigarette until evening. Outside, roosters seem to argue with an amplified call to the day's first prayer from the mosque downtown. Within a half hour, the family retreats to the bedrooms for two or three more hours' sleep. I wriggle back over to my mat, and Mohammed's mother flicks off the light.

Today Mohammed works another infrequent morning shift with his UNRWA partner, allowing us another chance to visit and photograph in Canada Camp Palestine this afternoon. He'll get eight days of vacation at the beginning of March, he says, and we both look forward to spending most of it in Canada Camp.

In the morning, men on the street ask me if I am fasting, often with a twinkle in their eye. I'm trying it today, so yes, I say, and they smile. But by the time I meet Mohammed I feel dull. Ramadan days, especially in the first week, can be psychological black holes, grinding expanses of hours lived in low gear, back up to full speed only with the *athaan*, or call to prayer that begins the *iftar*.

After work, Mohammed reports he ran into Khalil Audeh. The news is the crew was not, after all, arrested by the Egyptian *mukhabarat*, but it took them all day to extricate themselves, and they rode in to Cairo a day late.

By the time Mohammed and I reach Tel el Sultan, Mohammed is shuffling, almost stumbling along one of Canada Camp's sandy streets, his eyes like slits. I may feel listless, but I'm not a two-pack-a-day smoker. "It's these first days that are so hard," Mohammed says, trying not to complain. I'm not sure we're in shape to pay visits. Who would be in shape to receive us?

Three *shabab* wave like dots from beneath an umbrella stuck into the open sand beyond the camp. Two long, warehouse-like

buildings of an Israeli settlement rise in the distance. Walking
in the sand, I'm suddenly much hungrier, yawning and craving
a nap, right here in the soft, sun-warmed sand.

The guys under the umbrella are no better off. We shake
hands and neglect to exchange names. A few more *shabab* spot
us and amble out until we are eight. Talk is limp and aimless.
After a few minutes, one man walks me to another dune overlooking the Jewish settlers' road.

"Don't take your camera," advises Mohammed. "Someone
might see you and begin shooting. You never know."

I ask my escort if kids ever come to this place to—and I
make a motion of throwing a stone.

"No, not here," he replies. "But sometimes when there is a
strike, the Jewish bosses come down this road and the workers
climb over this dune to meet them and go to work in Israel."
General strikes of one or more days are called by Palestinian
factions, sometimes separately, sometimes in coalition, to
commemorate dates in Palestinian history, and also to protest
individual actions of the army and Civil Administration. On a
strike day, motor traffic is prohibited and business is halted
except for doctors, bakers, journalists, teachers and students.

"Really? They break the strike by coming here?"

"Yes. It is officially forbidden by the *intifada*, but sometimes people understand a family needs money, needs the
work so badly, the *shabab* pretend they don't see the workers
coming here from all over Tel el Sultan and Rafah."

He suggests we walk no closer to the settlement. He says he
doesn't know its name. Nothing really exists, I think to myself,
until it is named.

Only when we return to Khan Yunis, with the *athaan* just
minutes away, does our energy pick up. We walk quickly now,
weaving through the market packed shoulder-to-shoulder with
men—they do the Ramadan shopping mostly—and dropping
into a sweets shop where Mohammed buys a bag of something
and I pick up a carton of candy bars for the kids. Ramadan is
treat month. We reach the back door just as the call spreads
over the camp like a magic wand, Cinderella's midnight in

reverse. The streets go empty and 75,000 people in Khan Yunis sit down and eat at precisely the same minute, and in every other town and every other camp it is exactly the same.

It is a bright morning when I walk up from the taxi stand on Sea Street to Mohammed's house again. Nearly a week has passed since I was last here. Rafah lay shackled under forty-eight continuous hours of curfew after the army shot to death a uniformed UNRWA nurse during a confrontation in Shaboura Camp. He was the fiftieth Gazan to die under fire since the December 17, 1992, expulsions of Muslim leaders. A three-day general strike followed to protest both the killing and the curfew. With Rafah inaccessible, I took care of photo lab work in East Jerusalem.

As I pick a path among mucky street lagoons, two young shop attendants with whom I've chatted several times run up to me.

"Did you hear? Did you hear?" says one, eyes wide.

"No, what?"

He speaks rapid Arabic and all I catch is "Tel Aviv" and "two dead" and "seven not dead" and "knife." He makes stabbing motions just in case I miss his point. He looks at me as if he's just told me his soccer team won yesterday's game.

I adopt a sober, journalistic bearing and inquire: the assailant was Gazan; it happened this morning. More *shabab* drift over. A tall, older one interrupts me in English, "Excuse me, but who are you and why are you here?" He is polite but serious.

I explain courteously. He asks for identification. I hand him my card from the Arab Journalists' Association in Jerusalem.

"I'm sorry to bother you," he says, handing it back, "but you know what we are afraid of." He walks away. I thank the two brothers for their news, shake hands, and continue up the street.

That night, Ahmed and Musa drop in after *iftar*. I've seen neither of them since Khaled's wedding two weeks ago, and they arrive in Musa's Mercedes taxi, the same one he nearly flew through the wet streets in pursuit of film for Omar's wedding. Ahmed has given up on his beard. "I don't want people to think I am a fundamentalist," he says when I comment. We sit with Mohammed, his brothers, and several friends in the living room, passing around tea, apples and *'atayif*, pancakes filled with ground nuts, fried and soaked in honey to the consistency of a heavy sponge. Musa snatches up two; I follow suit; Ahmed turns them down. "I don't like *'atayif*," he says, as desultory as old Eeyore in *Winnie the Pooh*. I look at him, overplaying surprise. He shrugs. "It is all we ever eat," he says. "It's new for you but for me it's so boring. Every Ramadan it is the same. I think in America you have more different foods to choose from?" He fires up a cigarette and everyone laughs at him.

Conversation turns to the knife attack in Tel Aviv. I ask opinions. "I do not support this killing of civilians," Ahmed says. "It will bring us more problems from the army. Like revenge. But it is a sign about how much desperation there is here in Gaza. Like a cry for help."

Musa argues. "Killing civilians is wrong, yes, but look at how they kill our children all the time! They destroy our houses, like Amal! They do this to us, ordinary people. Every day they are doing this!" Ahmed nods; Musa lights a cigarette, adding, "And we cannot forget our land. My family had a nice farm and now we are in this camp. Why? Why are we here?"

As curfew nears, Mohammed and I steal final moments of companionship by escorting Ahmed, Musa, and a friend of theirs, Marwan, down Sea Street, into the camp. It's windless and silent on the empty boulevard; we hear our own steps crunch in the dust.

Marwan is a bookish young man I've met only tonight. He speaks quietly in English, below a level the others can hear.

"Next time," he says, "I want to ask you about love. There is an experience, something I want to tell you."

"Sure," I reply. "Will you visit the house again?"

He nods and he doesn't let on more.

His request rips a cold tear in the shroud that occupation wraps around life here. Everything is politics, politics, just as

Raji the carpenter in Canada Camp said. I don't talk after I hear Marwan. The moon is sliced in half tonight, our only light, since every street lamp was long ago smashed by *intifada* stones. The conversation behind me now is warm and dances like a campfire. We are shadows gliding in the dust, each of our fifteen minutes until curfew savored as preciously as foreknowledge of the moment of death. Mohammed and Musa hail another cluster of shadows. How different from home, where I'd avoid packs of men on dark streets with justifiable fear. But not here. Here you call out to greet them. If you know someone, both groups shift course to cross the street, meet in the middle, shake hands all around and make introductions, saying peace be upon you, peace be upon you and would you like a cigarette?

On the first day of Mohammed's vacation, we prepare to make up for lost ground with a long series of interviews in Canada Camp Palestine based on photographs I've made. That evening, Mohammed invites me to an *iftar* he will cook himself at the Rimal home of his UNRWA Refugee Affairs Officer. "I love to cook," he says, "but at home my mother won't let me. She says it isn't customary. So I will do this there."

The villa is a giant white box, sealed from the street by a high white wall, one of few I've seen without graffiti. Inside it is sparely but elegantly furnished: international RAOs are paid far above their Gazan counterparts. Jazz floats from a portable compact disc player. Wine glasses clink and I meet half a dozen men and women, all twentyish to thirtyish Europeans or North Americans, all RAOs. I am told I can name them in print using only radio code names, and I cannot quote them without UN approval. "Victor" is a gangly, gregarious, balding Dane who, with Mohammed, is calling the kitchen "a closed cooking zone," keeping the curious at bay with mock military authority.

In the velveteen chairs of the living room, shop talk is on one theme: today's killing of an Israeli Jew in Rafah. It is a very serious incident. One RAO arrived on the scene just minutes after she believes he died. He was an accountant for the Israeli gas company who drove, for reasons no one can fathom, from the Gush Qatif settlements in toward Rafah on the Tel el Sultan-Rafah road. His mistake was to do this in a car with a yellow Israeli license. This is something Israeli settlers in the Gaza Strip know perfectly well to avoid doing, she says.

Soldiers at the checkpoint at the edge of Gush Qatif told the RAO they had warned the accountant not to go beyond the settlement bloc, but he had insisted. *Shabab* must have spotted the car coming, noticed the plate, grabbed stones and struck in an instant. He lost control and smashed hard into the corner of a concrete wall at the edge of Block J, Rafah refugee camp, about a mile from Canada Camp. *Shabab* came running by the hundreds in minutes: it happened just after school let out. Several walked out of the crowd with automatic rifles, their faces masked. The driver never moved from his seat.

The RAO says the impact of the crash looked severe, and she couldn't tell whether he died before he was shot or not. Israeli officials, however, are already calling it an execution. But worse, she says, her mobile radio hadn't been working all day. She had to leave the scene to call an ambulance.

Now, three hours later, Rafah is under curfew for the second time in a week. The entire Gaza Strip has been sealed at its borders. There will be house-to-house searches for the *shabab* who stoned and shot the man. This, the RAOs agree, could drag the curfew out two, three or more days. Maybe houses will be blown up. There will be beatings and arrests. Settlers might seek their own revenge. Escalation, they say, is a virtual certainty.

Mohammed and Victor emerge announcing the dinner I'd nearly forgotten. It is long after *iftar*, but this is a non-Muslim house. Mohammed has been smoking and nibbling since sunset. Talk of brutality is abandoned with professional dispatch as we move to the polished dining room table with individual place settings. Mohammed serves fresh broiled fish, green salads, french bread and "spaghetti Mohammed," a delicious mess of baked beef and pasta. All but Mohammed accept another round of red wine. As we finish, the RAO who was in Rafah gets a call. It's brief. Her face tenses. She hangs up and walks over to her coat. The Civil Administration, she says, is insisting the man was alive when she arrived on the scene, and that her story of her radio malfunctioning is a coverup for her deliberate neglect to call an ambulance because the man was Jewish. She must meet her director at once to plan a response. The others are sympathetic but unsurprised: Israel, they say, hates the RAO program because of its international witness to army violence against unarmed civilians.

"So Dick," Mohammed says, putting his arm around me as I leave, "you know we like to eat like this when we can, even when things are so bad because this is our life here. We will see about the situation in Rafah tomorrow, but I do not think we can go to Canada for some days. Remember Ramadan can be like this."

I sleep fitfully, filled with half-dreamed schemes to photograph Canada Camp under curfew.

To support the extended household, the four adult women in Mohammed's family share: daily laundry; twice-daily floor sweeping and mopping; food shopping and preparation of the three daily meals; care for eight children; tea and snack preparation for visitors; and breadmaking two or three times weekly. One supplements the family income with part-time work outside the home.

CHAPTER 8
CURFEW

The next day, inside UNRWA's high-walled Gaza city compound, my pleas to ride into Rafah under UN auspices are turned down, even when I promise to leave my cameras behind. Outside the director's office I find an RAO who tells me he was in Rafah in the early morning. At least 500 soldiers are on patrol in the streets, he estimates. "It's more tense there now than anything I've seen in the nine months I've been here," he says.

"How can I get in?" I implore. He shakes his head, saying without UN identification it would be somewhere between "really dangerous" and "really stupid" to even try.

I spend the day reading in Rimal. In the evening I head south to Khan Yunis, where I play with the kids through *iftar*, and a few friends of Mohammed visit. There is less laughter and joking than usual tonight.

After curfew, I am bouncing three-year-old Hosam about the living room on my shoulders when we all hear the guns. We stop and freeze to listen in the ritual now growing familiar. I let Hosam down; he and the other kids look over at Mohammed and the men. It's not close. After several dozen shots, it ends in less than half a minute. Mohammed guesses it was near the middle of town, and it was an exchange between guerrillas and soldiers, because several different types of guns sounded.

Jeeps are easy to hear after curfew: there's no other traffic. We peer through slits in the corrugated metal of the pantry: the first one skids to a halt up at the corner of Sea Street. Ten others—we count them carefully—raise dust as they pass the intersection in high gear. A stiletto searchlight probes method- ically from house to house. When it comes to ours, we pull back just inside the door. Rafat ascends the roof using a practiced, catlike maneuver up a makeshift ladder I'd not noticed before. Jeeps are surrounding our section of the camp, he reports. Ibtisam and Aysha corral children into respective family bedrooms and close the doors. The men stand watch from the pantry.

"They are cutting off the escape of the armed *shabab* who fired on them," says Mohammed. "They expect the *shabab* to escape into the snakeways of the camp. They will either wait for them to appear or begin searching houses. But we have heard no ambulance, which means probably no injuries in the shooting. So I think there will not be curfew in the morning."

"Mohammed," I ask, "have soldiers ever fired tear gas into your house?" This happens now and then in both the West Bank and Gaza Strip.

"No," he says. "Not inside. That is why this screen is here. But many times it hits the outside of the house, or lands on the roof. And for every time that happens or shootings or searches or even when *shabab* throw stones, there are ten or twenty times like this now. Just jeeps, as you see now, the searchlights and this fear we feel."

I make a note of it: the ordinary state of affairs.

The next hour passes in silence. There are no sounds of house-to-house searches. The jeeps do not move. We fall asleep cautiously. By the time the family stumbles in for *suhur* at 4:15 A.M., the jeeps have gone.

Rateb, Mohammed's elder brother, will be stuck home again today. The border with Israel at Erez checkpoint is closed for a third day. He still doesn't have a job, and today, he complains, he can't even go looking. "I may have to find work here in Khan Yunis that would pay half or less. The wage is better in Israel," he says.

By daybreak, the women are cleaning in the kitchen. Each foam mattress is draped on a line, beaten with a broom and left to air in the warming sun. Mohammed's mother sweeps and washes the smooth tile floor using rags wrapped about a dilapidated, long-handled squeegee. When she is finished,

Ibtisam takes the squeegee and does the same up in the men's living room. I phone in to the RAO office in Gaza city to beg again for permission to ride as a UN observer into Rafah.

"Sorry," the director tells me, his voice betraying irritation now. "Maybe when the curfew is over."

That would be completely useless, I think, hanging up abruptly, angry now. How can we photograph daily life in Canada Camp if we are here and not there, curfew or no?

A call to UNRWA's Public Information Officer is no more encouraging. "It's a hell of a curfew," he tells me. "Nobody's going to get you in there. I sure can't. Just wait it out."

I hang up, obsessed with made-for-TV fantasies of crawling into Canada Camp through orange groves, then bolting a final hundred yards across the open sand before the patrolling soldiers spot me and—what?—open fire? My imagination leads me to few endings other than trouble, but it persists. I sit with Mohammed in his bedroom, where he is waking from his post-*suhur* nap.

"Is there a way we—or I—could sneak in?" I ask. "I know reporters who have done this through even heavy curfews in the West Bank. Maybe there is someone who could take us. I'd pay them. I don't even have to photograph, I just want to see so I can write about it—"

Mohammed cuts me off. His voice has turned sharper than I've heard before. "This is really the life here, really, really, really! This is a good lesson for you! I am in favor of trying to go, but here in Gaza Strip, once you make the effort you must accept it is not possible. The one who does not do this ends up dead."

I let this soak in. He adds, "Just relax and try, try to enjoy the day. We can stay here at home. It will be so fine." He is, I remember, on vacation. I, however, am not. It doesn't feel fine at all, no, it feels like a dereliction of journalistic duty. And I can't take this arbitrary curtailment of freedom without a good fight. That would go against my upbringing. As I write this thought in my notebook, I realize at once that plenty of dead and imprisoned Palestinians have doubtlessly felt this way, too. My frustration suddenly seems rather inconsequential. In front of me I can picture everyone I've met in Canada Camp, Tel el Sultan: Hanan, her husband and their daughters; Mustafa, his wife and four kids; old Abd El Rahman in his barbershop; and Rowhi's littlest girl Rula, all braced, shuttered, imprisoned in their own homes, waiting only for the mind-shattering clatter of rifles and boots at the metal front door.

Over another cup of tea, I keep writing. A thought emerges that whatever Mohammed and I accomplish inside Canada Camp is likely to be less interesting than how we finally got there at all. If we do. I put a star on this page for later.

I look at Mohammed, drifting off to nap again, and surrender.

Out in the pantry, Ibtisam stuffs laundry an armful at a time into the bucket-sized, tiny portable electric washer while Suzanne holds baby Majd. Laundry for fifteen takes all morning this way. The sun pokes irregular blotches of warmth through the hanging clothes and metal. For the first time, I find myself making photographs of the two women freely. Mohammed joins us. We all take turns with the camera, and suddenly I find it's a pleasant morning after all.

In the afternoon, Musa drops by and suggests a walk to a friend's farm. We hitch a ride on the passing UNRWA teacher's bus, and when we get out, it is quiet. Down a dirt lane on the outskirts of Khan Yunis, beneath an arbor bisecting fallow expanses of grass, air from sea and field hangs unspoiled, as rich as a meal to my empty, Ramadan stomach. No stench of sewage. Palm trees eclipse the sun, silhouettes exploding shadows out of light. Everything comes in greens and blues, not the dun browns and grays of the camps. Faint bleats and jingles from sheep, riffles of leaves and far-off yelps of children only accent soft, ageless quiet.

Musa's friend is not home. We circumnavigate a few fields, some striped with plastic irrigation tubing, others furrowed with damp irrigation channels. Nine out of ten gallons of Gaza Strip water gets used this way. All of it comes from one underground aquifer, and so overpumped is this that water throughout the Gaza Strip tastes salty as the sea seeps in to redress the imbalance. Salinity is at least a growth retardant to crops here, and sometimes a killer. Only a few wells still pump *maaya helwa*, "sweet water," anymore. Since 1967 the only new wells drilled in the Gaza Strip have served Israel and its eighteen settlements, although in that time the Palestinian population has doubled.

Except for tomatoes and cabbage and cucumbers, none of us can name the crops we pass, even though both Mohammed and Musa are the sons of men who were farmers before they became refugees. I find our ignorance pitiable. Agriculture was the heart of the coastal Palestinian economy for 4,000 continuous years, until it was surpassed by day-worker industrial jobs in Israel in 1967. Long ago, in the centuries of the annual camel caravans from North Africa to Mecca for *hajj*, or pilgrimage, these fields filled the silos of the Red Sea port of Aqaba and thus fed hundreds of thousands of pilgrims. These fields fed travelers from every country of the Old World who passed on the busy Egypt-Palestine road; they have also fed— and been plundered by—the more than forty armies that have marched through this corridor between the continents. Figs, dates, almonds and olives; oranges, lemons, apples and watermelons; wheat, barley, corn and dozens of vegetables: all have grown abundant from these sandy soils and now, we don't even know what we are looking at. We catch a Peugeot taxi back home for *iftar*, and the sight of the camp comes like a shout in the middle of a dream.

At the meal, there are a half dozen guests, so men and women eat in separate rooms. The television room goes to the women, and the upper living room goes to the men. We are twelve: the brothers Mohammed, Rateb, Khaled, Rafat; friends Yunis, Khaled, Abed and myself; and boys Ahmed, Sharaf, Sherif and Hosam. It's a gregarious gathering, a romp in fields of conversation, as if we never really quite ended our afternoon walk. I notice how my confinement to Khan Yunis, thanks to the daily difficulty of getting to curfewed Rafah, is turning into a sense of belonging right here. On our walk today, Mohammed explained less to me than usual. He doesn't need to now. He is less the guide, and I am less the curiosity. Together, we have grown more into equals.

On March 6, Saturday, Mohammed and I squat on the curb and roll dice on his neighbor's backgammon board. Rafah is under twenty-four-hour curfew for a fourth day. Up north, Erez checkpoint is still shut down, too, though rumor has it Monday it will be reopened. The Strip is quiet also because today is the first of the two monthly general strikes memorializing the *intifada*, now entering its sixty-fourth month. Since 1988, the sixth and the ninth of each month recall December 6 and 9, 1987, the first days of the "shaking off." Until the Gulf War, the eighth, too, was a strike day. Once I commented to a Palestinian college student the strikes must hurt the scraggly Palestinian economy. "It is the only means of collective expression left to us," she had replied.

One of the RAOs drops by in his UN car while on his rounds. "How's Rafah?" I ask, hungry for information.

"We saw a few women shopping today," says the RAO's assistant. "They slip down the sides of the streets when the soldiers are out of sight, stepping into the nearest shop that keeps its door open just a tiny crack. One learns to recognize these cracks. They have to or the family would begin starving." Women take this risk, he continues, because they risk a stiff fine, but men risk beating and prison as well as a fine.

"But they are doing some unusual things today," he adds, referring to the soldiers. "They prevented doctors from going to work. I've never seen this before. It is against all the rules of curfews. They must be very angry about the dead settler."

Later, Marwan passes by and invites me for a walk. I haven't seen him since that night we walked on Sea Street and he made his cryptic comment about wanting to talk about love. The day hangs suspended between winter and spring, overcast now, neither cool nor warm. No cars pass us due to the strike. I keep one hand on a camera, but I don't find anything to photograph. He stoops slightly, and his eyebrows hang, like so many faces here.

"These customs of ours, you can't know how much I hate them," he says after we've discussed my work with Mohammed and his progress in school. "Remember I told you I wanted to say something about love, a kind of love story?"

"What happened?" I reply, remembering. Why does he want to talk to me about this, I wonder? Is it just something he can't speak of in society here?

"This girl, you know, and I, we grew up near each other. Just a few houses away. And we liked each other too much."

By now I know "too much" is the way many people say, "very much" in English.

"It was mutual? I mean, how did you know she liked you? Could you speak to her?"

"Yes, but it was so difficult. We had to wait for times when both of our families were gone, every person in both houses except the two of us. We would have like a secret meeting, watching out for neighbors, too. But this was only two or three times, because our families are such big ones. And then just to talk, you know? For a minute, maybe two minutes. I could never speak to her on the street, or in school, or anywhere. Nowhere. And now she is married."

"What?"

"Her family married her three years ago, while I was in prison."

"You were in prison?"

He looks at me and nods, but doesn't want to talk about it.

"So who did she marry?"

"One that her father arranged. She could say nothing."

"And she would have preferred to marry you?"

"Yes, I know this. But I was in prison, and like I said, she could say nothing."

We are at the edge of the camp. We start up a long dune above two rectangles where boys play soccer. These fields, I hear, are, like everything else, divided by faction: the near one is for Hamas kids, the far one for Fateh. Another, further away, is for PFLP. An enormous, overflowing dumpster sits below. From here, the camp looks splattered on the gently rolling earth.

"So when you came back from prison, she was married," I say.

"Yes. It was worse than the feeling of being in prison when I heard this. I was so angry, but I could say nothing either. It is all like pretending. She lives in Rafah now. I think she has a baby."

"Do you ever see her?"

"Sometimes in the market, if I am in Rafah, but if I do I turn and go another way. It is too difficult because we cannot ever speak to each other. Never. And who else is there for me? It is too difficult here to meet a girl, to talk with her. Always it is someone arranged by the family. I hate this. It should be no problem for a man and a woman to sit with each other, to talk, in the street or anywhere. I know it is easy. I learned this, you know, when I came back from prison. Then so many people came to my house to congratulate me, and girls, too."

"And you could talk to them then?"

"This was like an exception made by the *intifada*. But it was no problem to talk to them. But after those days, nothing. I cannot talk to any of them anymore. What am I supposed to do? Everyone in Gaza Strip is in my position. I don't want to marry someone I don't choose. I want to marry only for love. For this reason I think I will not become married, ever. Not unless I can leave. I want to go to America, or Germany. But I will need a visa, and how can I get this?"

Now he is making circles in the sand with his hand. I don't want to explain how difficult U.S. visas are again. I stay quiet, and he doesn't pursue the topic.

"I like to think she still likes me," he says. "But how will I ever know now? I think sometimes it is just my imagination anymore."

CHAPTER 9
A WORLD OUT OF BALANCE

In the morning, I phone Mohammed from Rimal. "The curfew's up in Rafah," I say. "We can go now."

He agrees slowly, more warily than I've heard before. "The day after a curfew is even more tense in Ramadan," he says. "If we are stopped, we will pretend not to know each other. Everyone will be so angry at the army for the curfew, and the soldiers will not like to see a journalist today."

Muraj checkpoint is clogged. Every car undergoes pinpoint inspection today. But a hundred yards before the checkpoint, our Mercedes driver turns onto a dirt road and navigates a bypass between farms. I am shocked the army neglects this obvious path around the checkpoint; I am relieved, though. Everyone thanks the driver as our tension slacks, and he returns us a satisfied grin. Just before Shaboura Camp, as we crest a hill, the monochrome figures are there in front of us again, waving to stop, hard brakes, and now it won't be so easy: a special checkpoint has been set up here, just for today. Six soldiers line each side of the pavement and at once goosebumps crawl up my arms like maddened ants. Around me, every face has gone rigid. Ahead, the soldiers lean and peer into each car. Papers pass back and forth through windows. I stuff my camera bag out of sight and adopt the blank face that hides adrenaline, disgust and fear.

Our turn. The first soldier registers our faces, one by one. He waves. Pass. Not even an ID check. A miracle in progress, I think silently. I sit straight to keep their line of sight low on my face that feels as white now as a searchlight. We pull out slowly, slipping past the rest of the squinting, khaki-clad faces.

Any moment I sense the miracle could end with a shout as one of the twelve will surely spot the foreigner, but none do. On the outskirts of Rafah, I am lightheaded. Mild shock. Another ordinary Gazan trauma to which I am not yet accustomed.

The Rafah market is, in contrast, a cauldron of human warmth. We maneuver our way slowly to the Tel el Sultan taxis: Mohammed knows half the population of this city, it seems, and after four days under curfew, everyone has a story. From within the shadow of a shop awning, I photograph soldiers who are using a rooftop as a watchtower over the market. Mohammed doesn't like it. "It is like they are inviting someone to throw stones at them," he says. "By standing there they will for sure provoke something."

In Canada Camp, Mustafa is overjoyed to see us, but to him, the day is full of ominous portents. "I want to tell you my opinion of this killing," he begins rapidly. We are his first visitors in four days. "The problem is we aren't a responsible people. This man was an accountant!" He looks disgusted. "They did not have to kill him. You know the *shabab* say there were about a thousand of them there in the minutes after it happened. Everyone heard it. And maybe 90 percent of these boys escaped to Khan Yunis, to Nuseirat, to anywhere to get out of Rafah. This lifting the curfew today is a trap to get them to come back home. But most of them will suspect this and stay away today. Rafah these days is coming into a very bad situation. I think by five o'clock they will put the curfew back again to trap the *shabab*." Mohammed and I register a glance. "You should leave no later than four o'clock," he continues. "In the last hour before *iftar* the market will be the most crowded, and that is when the soldiers may harass the *shabab* and attack."

Last Ramadan, he reminds us, it was in that hour one day an army jeep patrol chased several stone-throwing *shabab* into the Rafah market. The driver struck and injured a seventy-year-old woman, and a raging crowd at once surrounded the patrol. The soldiers panicked and shot their way out. Four Gazans died and more than seventy were wounded; the soldiers escaped unhurt.

"When this curfew came, I was in Israel, working," Mustafa carries on, the edge on his voice sharpening. "We were allowed back because we had our work permits. But we didn't have time to buy food, and my kids were in tears the whole first night as we didn't have anything. And it is Ramadan, when we should be having such nice meals and nice visiting. We couldn't even go to the mosque, and if you are not a Muslim you can't even imagine this feeling."

"You mean you don't keep a stock of food for curfews?" I ask. I'd thought this was as routine in the Gaza Strip or West Bank as keeping tea on hand for visitors.

"No," he says, perhaps a bit embarrassed. His tone keeps me from asking whether it was poverty or oversight. "And on the second day my wife was able to get some food from our neighbor. That was also the day the soldiers searched the houses here in Canada Camp. They didn't beat or arrest anyone here, but they searched every room and asked questions." He mocks a soldier's voice: "Were you there at the accident? What do you know about it? Do you have anyone from outside your family here? Guests or relatives? Many, many questions. You know, at least in Canada Camp Egypt we did not have to live with this."

We leave at the time Mustafa suggests. Mohammed is tense, fearful of getting caught in a new curfew. The market crowd is fuller now as the hour for *iftar* approaches. Our Peugeot hits gridlock. We step out and Mohammed at once questions passersby.

"Everyone is saying they expect soldiers any minute," he tells me. "If they start shooting here now it will be to kill, not at the legs, believe me. Some may want revenge for the settler. But I hope not, so much I hope not."

Still, we shake hands with a few men and exchange strained smiles, keeping our eyes alert from side to side.

Behind us, a commotion, and then urgent shouts of "*Jeish! Jeish!*"—"Army! Army!" The scattering is frantic but not quite all-out panic. That might come with shots. Mohammed grabs my hand. "Hold on," he commands. "If they come and we go into the snakeways I would run faster because I know it so well. This way we stay together."

His loyalty moves me. I hold on.

He yanks open the front door of another Peugeot taxi that's honking through the running crowd like a frightened goose. We roll into the seats at a jogging pace. At the edge of the crowd, with our escape route to the Khan Yunis taxi stand clear now, we climb out. No shots yet. "Maybe we can stay a few moments?" I ask, catching my breath and cinching lenses onto two cameras.

The crowd is slowing down. We can't even see any soldiers. Like a wave that washes up and back, the crowd has stopped and has begun to drift toward the market again. Through the long lens, however, I see it is only the men returning. And boys are massing at the other end, a quarter mile away, near the soldiers.

Tear gas thuds from guns somewhere beyond the *shabab*. It's a dull sound, like a paper bag popping, nothing at all like a bullet's crack. "I think it would be good to go now," says Mohammed. "If there is a confrontation they could declare a curfew in a few minutes for all Rafah, and we must be past the checkpoint by then."

We turn for a taxi, but the stand is suddenly deserted. We look around: cars are gone from every street. More shouts of "Army!" go up; three more tear gas canisters, pop-pop-pop, I still can't see them and the crowd is in flight around us once again. We don't say anything to each other.

Then, right in front of us, like a mythic white whale slipping from a coral cave, the UNRWA teachers' bus heaves its rectangular bulk out of a tiny camp alley, obliviously setting out on its regular daily run from Rafah to Gaza via Khan Yunis. We hail the driver. He recognizes Mohammed—of course—and, cloaked in the relative immunity of the United Nations, we are waved out first through the special Shaboura checkpoint, and then through Muraj. When I step off into the throbbing market at Khan Yunis, I feel like we've just escaped into a free country.

At *iftar* I tell Mohammed I wish we could have stayed to photograph the confrontation. "I can't believe I haven't been able to do this yet," I say, not letting on to the depth of my photojournalist's frustration.

"Look," he says, "what we saw today was very significant if you are looking for things that are typical and not exceptional here. You saw nearly everyone run away from the market. So you learn from this it is only a few who join the confrontations in these days, not like before, when they did not shoot so much." After all, this is, he reminds me, our goal together: a depiction of the life that is called ordinary.

In the night I dream of the occupation. Soldiers and crowds and panic and I get shot with a miniature bullet, but I argue with the soldier afterwards and I don't die. At *suhur* I tell Mohammed and ask how often he dreams such things.

He laughs. "I think for most of us here this is the main thing we dream, all the time," he says. "This is a psychological problem for us, especially the children. They are scared all the time. We grow up not knowing what it is like not to be frightened."

He pauses and looks at the bread, jam and sliced egg. "You know Ibtisam and I, we have an agreement not to talk about dreams, not ever. If we were to share these things we would only frighten each other more. Because for us, our dreams often involve our children, and there are so horrible things, we cannot think of them in the day."

By sunrise Radio Monte Carlo reports twenty-four-hour curfew was imposed in Rafah yesterday only in Block J, the neighborhood of the March 2 killing. Thus we can, conceivably, visit Canada Camp for the last day of Mohammed's vacation. But a Jewish settler was stabbed to death yesterday in Gush Qatif, the southern bloc of twelve Jewish settlements. Enraged settlers with automatic weapons have blockaded the main highway and gunned down a Palestinian at Erez checkpoint up north, which closed again after opening for only a

few hours in the morning. The 30,000 workers in Israel will
return tonight to face sniping gangs of settlers unless the army
clears them out, which no one expects it to do.

In the house, agitation is rising. Eight-year-old Ahmed
keeps interrupting Mohammed and me violently; his mother
yells at him to stop yet he continues.

"So we can go to Canada Camp," I say. "We can go around
Block J, right?" We have to go, I think, and do one interview
using photographs, just to feel some progress on our work.

But Mohammed fears vengeful settlers. At about one
o'clock we leave, more reluctantly even than yesterday.
Mohammed insists I leave all cameras at home.

Unexpectedly, the checkpoints are easy, but the Rafah market, so full yesterday, is gone, desolate, strewn with wood and
big shards of metal.

"The soldiers didn't come until after the *athaan*," says one
man. "They broke a few carts, harassed people, and shot three,
but none died. So today we have a strike in Rafah." The
wounding of three is not, apparently, a sufficient number to
alter the casual tone of his voice.

Another man offers to drive us to Canada Camp in his private car. Block J covers about twenty acres, and spans the main
Rafah-Tel el Sultan road. Therefore we must detour through
Shaboura Camp, where the twisted rails of the Cairo-Jaffa railroad, abandoned since the 1967 war, rise like a post-apocalyp-
tic sculpture flanked by the most ragged of all the Strip's cinder
block huts. Figures wander in dust. "Fateh-land" this is called:
the poorest of the camps is also, not surprisingly, the strong-
hold of the militant *sokour fateh*, the Fateh Hawks.

It takes an hour to get to Canada Camp via the crowded
one-lane road. Now, this all that links the 10,000 people in Tel
el Sultan with the rest of the Strip. Hanan's face is drawn and
sober. Her living room is, however, as spotless as ever.

"I think it is not good for you to be here today," she says.
"From one hour to the next we don't know what will happen."

All talk is about "the situation." The fear of settler violence
escalating into a massacre is palpable. She and Mohammed

discuss events, times, places, interpretations and harbingers. At 3:30 we hail a ride out from a lone, desperate, strike-breaking taxi driver, and endure another stomach-thumping traverse around Block J and back to Khan Yunis. I spend the evening with a splitting headache.

In the morning, Israeli fighter jets crack open the low sky above Khan Yunis every few minutes. They fly just below the speed of sound in a piercing crescendo whistle that at the instant of passing explodes into a concussive, shattering roar. The ground trembles and the resonance is felt in the gut. I hadn't read of this kind of collective punishment before.

The noise sets baby Majd screaming unattended in the bedroom. Mohammed, amazingly, sleeps on. Must be a Gazan skill, I think as I break my note-writing to go hold Majd. Writing is hopeless anyway. The older kids are agitated and hyperactive, and they keep bothering me. Ibtisam thanks me for holding the baby. She looks weary and drawn and says she won't be going out to work today, but doesn't say why. Her work with the kids is consuming, and the social distance between us still feels huge. Rateb tells me he heard Block J is under curfew again today, the seventh out of the last eight days.

Later we sit outside on stray cinder blocks and upturned plastic buckets. We lean back against the corrugated sheeting, stretch our feet in the dust, and watch the sunlight cut shadows as the jets tear up the sky: Mohammed, me, and a shifting band of kids, brothers, neighbor men and passing-by-saying-hello men. Conversation rides in idle, today being another strike day, the ninth, the second monthly commemoration of the *intifada*. With Erez checkpoint to Israel closed again, nobody is even trying to sneak out for a day's work. The listless boredom that is occupation's less noticed face sets in, and I grow restless.

A siren cries up on Sea Street. Our heads turn in unison. The ambulance, which looks like a delivery van painted white, leans into the corner, headed for the hospital. Another follows.

"See," says Mohammed. "They are coming from the south road, so there must be confrontations in Rafah or Shaboura."

An hour later, an RAO with whom Mohammed had tried to arrange a ride for us to Canada Camp today calls with regrets. She's stuck in the Rafah clinic because there are so many wounded, probably twenty-five or thirty, all live ammunition leg wounds, she says, no fatalities yet. She says all this like "Sorry, dear, I'm swamped at the office today."

The news makes me stir-crazy. The site of our story is going through convulsions and we are stuck on this filthy street just five miles away. I insist we at least go to the hospital. Mohammed seems more interested in trying to ignore all this on the last day of his vacation. I can hardly blame him. I hope I don't sound like a war tourist.

Nasser Hospital, which serves all of south Gaza Strip, is small, decrepit and as clean as the overworked staff can keep it. It is also mobbed. There are no restrictions on visitors. Before we find *shabab* from Rafah, in a dim upstairs hallway, amidst a crowd, we spot Rowhi, Mohammed's former supervisor at the Rafah Social Welfare Office.

"My brother, Adil, he was shot today," Rowhi explains, looking like he should be sitting down. "But he is okay, thanks be to God, it is just in his leg."

Adil seems about twenty-five. He is wrapped in a clean sheet and blanket and plugged into an IV tube. Nine other men fill the ward, each surrounded by friends or family that help the tiny hospital staff. "It's just like a sharp aching now," says Adil, pointing to his left thigh under the blanket. "They got it out whole, thanks be to God. M-16."

It's not so bad, Rowhi explains, because Adil was sitting on a chair in a Shaboura Camp pharmacy while a confrontation took place a few blocks away. This is usually a safe distance. "Then, 'boom!' a bullet smashed the window and went into his leg," he tells us. "It was from far away, though, so it did not hit the bone."

Mohammed buys Adil orange juice from a vendor outside. Ramadan fasting is waived for the wounded. Adil keeps muttering, "Praise be to God, praise be to God." Mohammed and I stay at his side until the sunset prayer. Rowhi says he'll stay through the 9:00 curfew.

The next morning I leave Mohammed's for another day of photo processing in Jerusalem. The day seems calm and close to rain again. As the Mercedes taxi from Khan Yunis to Gaza wheels out onto the main road, a southbound driver leans out his window toward us. "Settlers! Settlers in the road!" he cries, making frantic pistol-shooting motions with his hand. Our driver ducks the car onto another single-lane dirt track packed with every car that would normally travel the four-lane highway. Word is the main road has been closed by sniping settlers. The army is doing nothing to stop them.

By nightfall I am in Jerusalem for my lab work. I walk and walk in a cool drizzle along lit cobblestone streets on the Jewish west side of the city, astounded and relieved at the feel of freedom. No fear of an army here; no boys shouting demands to be photographed. I buy a slice of carryout pizza and feel lonely, like I did back in Cairo, as if I've abandoned friends in a time of need.

The next night I phone Mohammed for greetings and news.

"We are all fine, but the situation is so bad," he says. "Today there is another settler killed. A woman this time."

Oh no. "Where?"

"You know the Rafah checkpoint? Not far from there. She was picking up workers to take them to a job. One of them murdered her with a hatchet."

I'm quiet for a moment. "I'm sorry," I say, meaning it, for everybody now.

When I return the following afternoon, both Khan Yunis and Rafah are under twenty-four-hour curfew. Mohammed is back at work, and, using his curfew pass, he's managed to line up a ride home for us in a UN van from UNRWA in Gaza city.

Soldiers wave us past their jeep blocking the way into the Khan Yunis curfew zone. Further on, I am shocked not to see any soldiers on patrol. In fact, I see people standing outside door-ways, and even boys playing soccer in the traffic-less road.

"How can they be outside like this?" I ask Mohammed.

"They are being very careful. If they see or hear the jeeps they will disappear. Like the cat and the mouse. Each curfew is different. Yesterday, here there were so many soldiers, and no one went out then. And in Rafah, now in Block J, it is so strong, too. You will not see people like this there."

At the top of Mohammed's street a tire burns, a smoke signal for war. A handful of early-teens *shabab* circle it holding rocks, looking serious about defying curfew. We watch from the house, but the army declines the challenge. The tire smolders out, darkness gathers, and the *shabab* slip home.

We watch movies all evening. Rafat borrowed a VCR and rented two cheap and very gory action films today.

"In curfew?" I look at him, genuinely astounded.

He grins a trickster's smile and raises his eyebrows mischie-vously, keeping his methods to himself. "It is not a tough cur-few today," he shrugs. I shake my head in wonder.

After some sleep, *suhur* comes far too quickly. We sit on the cold floor, chewing bread and cheese and jam like somnambu-lants. Mohammed's neighbor broadcasts live prayer chants through a deafening, distorted public address system rigged up to his roof. The roosters across the street go wild.

But the family keeps quiet, waiting, straining for another voice. The army always ends curfews between 3:00 and 4:00 A.M. so workers in Israel can get their lengthy commute under way.

Between prayers I detect something distant, garbled and mechanical.

"Continue. Continue," Mohammed translates. "They just say this one word. It is all they have to say."

In the room, no signs of emotion, just a slight tensing of Ibtisam's lips. Rateb hasn't been able to look for work for two weeks now. The kids will be confined to the house again for another day of boredom, tension, cabin fever and fear. Mohammed will leave for work, and I'd prefer to spend the day in quiet Rimal writing up notes and sorting new photos. After lengthy advice, I slip out through the back door. The curfew, technically speaking, does not apply to me because I carry a U.S. passport, but this is not a realistic consolation. I time my appearance into the eerily vacant street with careful precision to coincide with that of the few curfew-exempt UN professional workers who I see walking, too. Still, I feel like prey. Alone, I stand in the spot where the UN van should arrive at 7:20 noting doorways, snakeways and walls: cover. A small boy materializes in a doorway. His stare is flat, as blank as an apparition. He doesn't say hello back. He probably thinks I'm Israeli. Why else would someone who doesn't look Palestinian be standing about in curfew?

By 7:30, the van hasn't come. No soldiers have passed, either, but I figure my odds of remaining unseen are deteriorating by the minute. At the sound of a vehicle, I tense and pull back toward a snakeway. But it's an RAO car. I'm out.

The next morning, I awake in Rimal. I am finding I cannot spend more than two or three nights at a stretch at Mohammed's, as much as I have grown to love the family. Too many people, too much smoke and too much struggle with Arabic for one who was raised in a room of his own where everyone spoke English. I wish I could be tougher, but my attempts at this have lately only left me with unbearable headaches. I also find that hours and days in Rimal have become essential to good notetaking and careful examination of photographs.

I return to Khan Yunis in time for *iftar*. The curfew ended this morning. As I step onto Sea Street from the taxi, a clump of men holler at me and wave me toward a back alley. Israeli soldiers on that roof there, they say, pointing. In front of that building, Sea Street is carpeted in stones.

"This is what they are calling 'O.P.,'" Mohammed tells me when I see him. "This means 'observation post.' All morning the *shabab* were here throwing stones. Look—see the soldier?" In a far-off, fourth-story windowframe of an unfinished concrete building, I register the helmeted figure.

"So what does this mean?" I ask, trying to make sense of it.

"I am afraid it is being considered a provocation. No one will like to look there and see these soldiers watching everything. And the soldiers they put up there are so few they themselves will be very afraid. It is like they are trapped by their own orders. They have put O.P.'s in most of the camps all over Gaza Strip today," Mohammed says.

We try to visit Canada Camp and spend the night at Rowhi's. We savor a massive *iftar* of chicken, rice, falafel, soup, salad, hummus, bread and a buttery cake. The meal calms me and seems to content the kids. Rula plays with her older brother, her two-year-old's memories of soldiers at the door faded, I hope, at least until next time.

In Canada Camp later, bare bulbs on extension cords silhouette the drapery of a tent in one dark and sandy street. Men sit on wicker stools in long rows. No interviews tonight: the head of a family I have not met before has died of old age. I sit with Samir, who tells me he is a relative of the deceased. He lives in Rafah town and labors in Israel when he can, he says. In a conspiratorial voice, he tells me he worked in Israel over the last strike day. I lift my eyebrows and ask how.

"You know," he chuckles, "I went with the others over to the road, the Jewish road over there." He waves toward the settlements. "There were many of us, a couple hundred. And then," he leans in, eyes widening, "in the curfew the next day I had to stay in Isdud, because we couldn't come back, you know, and there we all went to a club, you know, a night club and oh man!" He's grinning. "But it's so illegal to stay overnight in Israel like that. It made me very nervous, really. But it is so bad now, you know, we have to break some rules just because no one has money any more, and it was like some fun," he finishes, his voice flattening.

The night radio points out that fifty-seven Palestinians and ten Israelis have died violently in the past three months, the highest toll since the *intifada* began. For Israelis, it is the highest three-month toll ever. *El wadd'a,* "the situation," hangs on Gaza with a chokehold now. It is nearly all anyone talks about. Ramadan has become a peripheral, joyless grind. Tomorrow, the seventeenth, will be yet another strike, this to express solidarity with the 415 expelled Palestinian Muslim leaders.

In the morning, we complete our second of what we hope will be at least a dozen photo interviews, what we have decided will be the core of our work in Canada Camp, but my spirits are low. Between Mohammed and myself, the morning has been awkward, and I don't know quite why. Rowhi pilots us through the strike-empty streets in his UN Citroen to the Social Welfare Office, where hundreds of stir-crazy boys pack the normally abandoned yard. They've been displaced from a school in Block J, now suffering its fifteenth day of round-the-clock curfew. It's drizzling and cold. I'm exhausted yet again from the tension and the four A.M. *suhur.* I have to be in East Jerusalem tonight to shoot an assignment I've promised to a U.S. magazine, but I don't even know how I'll get there in the strike. But at the same time, I can't stand it here any longer. The boys climb the barred windows by the dozen and stare at me, saying "What is your name?" over and over in English as if I'm Exhibit A in their private zoo. The men around me talk *el wadd'a:* big confrontation at the O.P. in Khan Yunis today, many injured already, more this afternoon, for sure.

Mohammed packs me off on the UNRWA teacher's bus and seems relieved to be rid of me. "Every time there is news like this we all think, 'Was one of my sons hit? One of my brothers?' Every time. It is normal," he says. A guest is probably too much today. This afternoon, he returns to work. And it's not just any old job, I remind myself: he may be in the midst of battle in a few hours. But he doesn't explain in detail and I'm too tired to understand much. I tumble into a seat, morose, amazed that all 800,000 Gazans haven't gone stark raving mad years ago.

In Khan Yunis, blocks from Mohammed's house, men in the front seats cry "Army! Confrontation! Take the other street!" The driver reacts quickly by reversing and weaving through another alley. We swing onto Sea Street and I notice the crowd. I'm too tired for professional detachment; the sight revolts me. Everyone faces the five-story concrete shell of a building, the commandeered Observation Post. Dozens of *shabab* line the edges of the street, nobody too far from cover. No stones and no shots now, but the ground in front of the building is salted with the white of rocks again. How, I ask myself, can soldiers on a fifth-story roof feel threatened by stones thrown from ground level? An ambulance crouches, its red bubble rotating steadily, waiting, a modern barge across the river Styx, just for Gazans.

I am tempted to yell stop, I want off. At last, a confrontation I could photograph. Then cautionary voices wrap me fast: I'd be without transportation in the strike; I'd be alone, with no guide where soldiers hold a high sniping position—and remember Mohammed's warning about a photographer maybe being the first target for a long-range "accident"; I'd jeopardize my Jerusalem assignment; and all this on a day where my own mental condition is nothing short of abysmal. I keep to my seat. Everyone else keeps to theirs, too. I have time for only one photo from the ignominious vantage point most Gazans seem to prefer around confrontations these days: from a safe distance, for a brief moment, in retreat.

CHAPTER 10
THE KILLING STREETS

Jerusalem once again becomes my refuge from the Strip's abuse of mind, heart and body. I had scarcely guessed, after those first weeks in January when everyone appeared to cope with *el wadd'a* rather admirably, how the fear can dig in so and consume every moment, how it can demoralize so quickly and completely. The word "occupation" no longer calls up the right images: *halat harb*, "state of war," is more accurate. I think about this as my magazine assignment secludes me for two days within the mustiness of a medieval library in the heart of the Old City. With each dawn I photograph narrow, stony streets to sound of church bells and the clatter of carts.

Gaza dominates the news these days. It's overwhelming, really, and easily desensitizing. In the past four days at least 150 young Gazans have been wounded by snipers on the fifth floor of the Khan Yunis Observation Post. Ten more families in the central Strip town of Deir al Balah listened as artillery made rubble of their homes following another search for activists. Another Israeli army jeep was ambushed by guerrillas; another soldier died. In Rafah, an attempted assassination of the visiting Dr. Haidar Abd Al Shafi, head of the Palestinian bilateral negotiating team, took the life of a popular UNRWA teacher. Witnesses said Israeli soldiers fired; the army, however, pointed the finger at the rejectionist PFLP. On television, Israeli citizens are hearing a call to arms to protect against knife-wielding Gazans. Lines, the newscasters say, are forming outside gun shops.

A newspaper poll announces 53 percent of Jewish Israelis want the Israeli army to withdraw from the Gaza Strip, and only 34 percent oppose this. But there is no public talk of it from high levels these days. This is unbearably discouraging. On March 22, *The Jerusalem Post* reports the Prime Minister, who cut short a trip to Washington to cope with the crisis, will respond by dispatching 1,550 more police to the Strip.

By the time I return to Khan Yunis, the *shabab* have given up protesting the O.P. Handfuls of soldiers now keep Sea Street's traffic under baleful watch from not one but, now, three O.P.'s, each commandeered from private homes with strategic views. But it is the last day of Ramadan, and tomorrow is the *eid al fitr*, the feast of fast-breaking, one of the two most significant holidays of the Muslim year.

Mohammed isn't home. I drop in on the teenage brothers in their Sea Street kebab shop to see what they can tell me.

They insist on plying me with an orange soda, on the house, laughing, saying, "Go on! You're not Muslim!" I accept, and then soberly ask about the week.

The jumpy, wiry one whistles, rolls his eyes and shakes his head. The quiet, chubby one says, "I saw everything!" and makes motions of throwing stones. For a moment I'm distracted by what I spot around his neck: a spent bullet hung on a black thread.

"It's from him," he says, motioning to his brother. "He goes to all the confrontations. Not me," he tisks.

The wiry one yanks up his pant leg to show me a scar, and then points to the pendant bullet. He doesn't stop there. He bares one scar after another, making sure I register each one until I understand he's been shot on six separate occasions. His proud grin is a demand for commendation.

I call him *mujahid*, struggler, and shake his hand, restraining astonishment and sadness: in an army he'd be a six-medal vet, and he can't be more than eighteen.

He beams at me.

I ask why there is a huge Palestinian flag spanning the alley next to their shop within plain sight of the O.P. "I thought soldiers harassed and arrested people for putting up a flag."

With pride and honor
With the life-pulse of all martyred revolutionaries
Our martyr
The hero
Maher Naim Al Majayda
                    —*translation of the poster,*
                              Khan Yunis,
                         March 22, 1993

"There was a martyr," the quiet one says. "So they leave it alone for a few days. Look there—" he points to a nearby young man—"he knew him."

The teenager, overhearing, ambles over.

"Who is the martyr?" I ask.

"Maher," he says.

"When?"

"Saturday afternoon."

"How old was he?"

"Eight."

I raise my eyebrows.

"Come on, do you want to visit his house? Lots of people are there." I thank the brothers and follow.

A "martyr house," or *beit shaheed*, is, like other funerals, held for three days. In this time, men and women visit separately, and in droves. The setup, like last week's smaller wake in Canada Camp, resembles a wedding. This is intentional, especially for martyrs, who in death are bonded with God so closely the only earthly metaphor is marriage. The martyr is celebrated and the father congratulated: his son has fulfilled one of the highest of aspirations, the giving of life for the just struggle of his people. I quickly ask the young man what I should say as we approach the line of men who have now turned to look at me, the stranger with a camera.

"Say, 'This is from Allah and may our God give you patience.'"

I quickly memorize the Arabic. Three rows of the little webbed stools line the sandy alley, too narrow for any cars. Flags droop against the unpainted concrete walls, limp along strings arcing from one shuttered window to the next. Posters, written by hand in fluorescent markers, bear spontaneous eulogies by the dozen.

My escort and I begin shaking hands with the long line of men who rise like a wave to greet us. Faces are grim. I am uncertain how to act. I say what I've been told, over and over. The group seems to hover somewhere between the ideal of celebration and an emotional reality of shock and grief.

I am installed on a stool against a plain wall. At least fifteen men surround me, men who want very much to tell their stories. I pull out my notebook to let them know I'll be as serious about listening as they about talking. Maher's father comes and squats next to me on the sand, his unshaven chin all the way down on his knee. He finds it hard to talk; he stares at the ground.

The group tells me, in combinations of English and Arabic, that Maher Naim Al Majayda was in fact eight years old when he left his house Saturday around 3:00 in the afternoon. His mother had asked him to buy a bag of cookies from the usual shop across Sea Street. There was a lull in the day's confrontation so it seemed safe. I know the shop, I say. I've bought chocolate bars there for the kids in Mohammed's house. They nod and continue. When Maher was returning, a small group of very young boys had gathered. They began shouting "some things" at soldiers who were, at the moment, changing shift at the O.P. more than 100 yards distant. Probably not very nice things. A few began throwing stones, which, owing to the young ages of the boys, traveled only a few feet. Maher stood, watching. He reached into his sack for a cookie, and took a bite that he never finished.

At the same instant, a soldier in the patrol knelt, sighted, and pulled the trigger on his M-16 once. The bullet tore into Maher's mouth, exited at the top of his spine and he fell, dead. A man in the street rushed to the small, fallen form as the boys shrieked and scattered and a second shot exploded the air: he, the men say, should survive his chest wound.

My head is suddenly swimming in thoughts as they go on to describe the wound in three-dimensional detail and the bloody remains of the cookie in his hand. Why didn't I read about Maher in *The Jerusalem Post* this morning? His death passed unremarked in the press. If this is not news, then it is an ordinary, routine event for Khan Yunis. It is normal. Ordinary? Routine? How can this—I can't even hear what the men are saying anymore. I grasp for a name, something to nail this cruelty into an ethical context. Murder. Okay. What else?

State terrorism. I didn't want to use that word "terrorism," not ever in my notes, but there it is blaring away at me, organized by the Israeli army, tolerated and sanctioned by the Israeli electorate, ignored by the U.S. State Department and rationalized—when it isn't ignored—in the press.

"What nationality you?!" one man asks me, poking me out of my stupor with an aggressive finger and his fractured English.

"American," I say, bracing for what might come next. I'm used to it now; the pattern of replies speaks volumes.

"The bullets, all the bullets here, they were made in USA. Why? Why?!"

I take it as a rhetorical question and tighten my lips. I keep eye contact to urge him silently to continue.

"We are not against the USA," breaks in another with a plaintive passion, "believe me. But we want the justice! Where is the justice! From '48 to '93 the foreign journalists all support Israel. Always they show us as terrorists and Israel as democratic. But what is the reality here?"

I nod. Maher's father squats next to me, unspeaking. Someone from the back of the group passes forward a copy-machine poster with a snapshot picture of Maher. His father takes it, folds it neatly into quarters, and hands it to me. He rises, shakes my hand, and turns.

The men talk on, now belaboring more abstract points about how Americans don't understand what it means, for them, to bankroll Israel, how behind its public words U.S. diplomacy is rife with hypocrisy, racism and neocolonialism. Soon everyone is pointing out his own scars to me, a macabre show-and-tell of lumpy limbs, fingers that don't work anymore and one boy with crazy eyes from a rubber bullet to the head. After a few moments of earnestness I catch on they are actually trying to one-up each other in dark comedy. "Okay," I say, looking up from my notebook, "is anyone here *not* wounded by the army? Besides me?" At this we all laugh, throwing off tension and returning to the present and the living.

From behind us, a sharp commotion of voices comes at us and heads turn. I don't understand what was said. Then three or four explosions reverberate off the concrete walls, M-16s from somewhere. They sound like bombs to me, not being familiar with the sonic signatures of automatic weaponry. We adjourn without formalities to the edge of Sea Street. It's mobbed. Tonight will be the biggest *iftar* of Ramadan and everyone is buying whatever he or she can afford. But the shots have chased out the cars and women are ducking into doorways and the *shabab* have stopped and they line the sides of the street. Everyone is looking left. More shots and we spot a soldier walking toward the market through the intersection maybe 75 or 100 yards away. I dutifully snap on my longest lens, and a man whose name I never learn grips my shoulder and carefully escorts me out to where I can get a photo. The soldier's fire is covering for the rest of his six-man patrol behind him, but I don't see any stones, not anywhere. The *shabab* flow toward him like lava. He swings and fires down our street and everyone jumps back only to creep forward some more the next moment. He must be terrified, I think, watching hundreds close in on himself like this. An ambulance howls and the crowd parts instinctively. The patrol slips right into the center of the market square that must be packed with last-minute *iftar* shoppers. More shots, one by one, slowly, like dripping water, and then the crowd picks up to a furious run and my guide keeps his hand on my shoulder and I find a moment to thank him. A second ambulance hurtles by us, but I don't see anyone injured. My guide points to where the soldiers are now. I don't see them—my eyes don't know what to look for as his do—but at least they have left the main square. A few more shots caution the running *shabab* as the soldiers finish their retreat and then the crowd stops. They're gone.

A man toting a video camera jogs up to me, panting. "Journalist?" he says.

"Yes."

"Come with me, there may have been a martyr. I have a car. Quickly."

We run hard, splashing through three blocks of sewage puddles and weaving through the crowd of men. We pile into his beat-up white Peugeot. The videotape will go to Reuters, he says, and his name is Khaled.

He drives not so much toward Nasser Hospital as *at* it, with the intensity that comes out in journalists from adrenaline and from caring. He dodges startled humans. In a few blocks a gang of men rush the car, screaming something. We don't stop, but they all tumble into the back seat anyway, four of them, the car rounding the corner at a hard jog.

Now something about *shaheed, shaheed*, martyr and more old Peugeots appear out of nowhere it seems, all going the same direction in dusty panic on the narrow road not to the front of Nasser Hospital but behind it. Men run on the road. The fourth man in back can't even fully shut the door of Khaled's tiny car. He leans half outside, shouting, crying in anguish. Others shout back and hearing their words, he begins sobbing so hard I'm afraid he might fall out.

"This man's cousin, we think he is a martyr," says Khaled. Intensity is his only emotion.

We swing into a clear area of sand and grass walled by plain cinder blocks. The man on the edge leaps out and runs flailing to another Peugeot where a small crowd gathers, screaming "Who?! Who?!" as he runs.

I get to the car with Khaled and wiggle in at knee height to photograph. A man—a nurse?—sits in the back and the prone body of a young man—twenty years old?—lies wrapped in a bloody sheet. Pandemonium.

On the other side of the car an older man sobs, "My son! My son!" over and over as another man supports him by the shoulders.

"He is with God," I hear from over my head.

"Goodbye, martyr, goodbye," from another. I fix my shutter speed high for my own shaking hands.

Everything happens with the swiftness of a dream. Someone explains we must move quickly because if the army comes for the body, the burial will have to occur under military supervision, which would humiliate the family and mock the martyr's status.

Friends and relatives of the martyr, March 22, 1993.

The body is lifted into the arms of the father. Across the thin grass, he walks slowly, staring ahead, his face twisted and streaked, a paternal Pieta. The crowd follows in an impromptu procession, all of it men, not a woman among us, not even the martyr's mother, some shouting, some weeping, most silent and we don't walk more than a few dozen yards. We halt at a flat, unmarked slab on the ground like the floor of a small house. The limp weight in the sheet is lowered carefully by the hands of men into the subterranean darkness of the tomb, the special, big one for the martyrs of the *intifada*. After the men lay out the body inside, they heave a squarish concrete slab to cover the entrance. Then their hands tamp and carefully smooth the cool, sandy earth at its base. Someone reads from the Qu'ran. Everyone stands silent, unmoving except to blot tears or touch the hand or the shoulder of someone near.

Then it's over. Less than half an hour after he fell, Jihad Mustafa Jarboua, who Khaled now tells me was twenty-one, is buried. The crowd disperses. Friends will do their best to assist the family with the traumatic transformation of the *eid al fitr* celebration into three days of *beit shaheed*.

He was killed, Khaled informs me, by one of the dozen-odd shots fired into the market square, the ones I heard while photographing from Sea Street. We walk toward the hospital now, where he says there are some injured, too. It's just after 6:00. I can't believe it was forty-five minutes ago I was sitting on a stool outside the place I will now forever think of as Maher's house.

At the hospital, there is more pandemonium, more crowded halls tracked with sand and mud. The official count of injured is eighteen; I heard no more than twenty-five or thirty total shots. "This is nothing," Khaled comments. "You should have seen it last week."

I run into Musa inside. "The whole thing was to provoke us," he says. "It's common. They order a patrol to go there just at that time. Some stones get thrown, they shoot some *shabab* and leave. It is like to show us who is boss. Why else do they do this at exactly the most crowded market, on the night of our feast?"

A comment from a Gaza journalist last summer replays for

me as I stand in the hall and photograph the injured: "They are planting the seeds of hatred in our hearts."

Mohammed's family rises at five the next morning even though *suhur* is no more until Ramadan next year. The kids can't bear to sleep: this is the first and happiest of the three feast days, the day of presents—new clothes, toys and gummy sweets. They charge about like little engines unmuffled, howling and yelping. Little Sherif is marching round and round the kitchen in a new black shirt piping out a political faction chant, *"Shab-iy-ye! Shab-iy-ye!"* far too seriously for age four; Salah is waddling wrapped in a fluffy orange jumpsuit, screaming with random, two-year-old delight. All at 5:00 A.M. I rub my head and fold up my blankets, amazed at the energy in this family so early in the morning.

Breakfast begins with heavily salted fish, a thirst-inducing tradition following a month of prohibitions against drinking liquid during the day. Halfway through, Ibtisam's father drops by, fitted out in a spotless, powder-blue cotton suit. He's nearly eighty, in admirable health despite a pack or two of cigarettes a day. To each child he hands a shekel coin and gathers each one in for a strong, stiff hug, grinning like a shaven Santa Claus. My mind flip-flops between the present and yesterday, like a car crash that won't go away until my mind comes to terms with what really happened.

The sun is brilliant today; the air may even grow hot later. But Rateb, Mohammed's elder brother, seems cheerless. He slumps quietly in a chair while I hold his youngest son, baby Abed. "Today is not much like a feast," he says. "Too many martyrs and injured. We have new clothes for the kids, okay. But for five years, since the beginning of the *intifada* it's been like this. At the beginning there was hope. But now just too many families unhappy."

Mohammed must go to work. UNRWA, he says, expects the worst trouble of all today, and he and his colleagues are all on for double shifts. In the afternoon, Ahmed and Musa escort me to another *beit shaheed*. Another long Palestinian flag stretches across another narrow alley where the sunlight glints off another of Khan Yunis' meandering stripes of sewage.

Salaam Shurab, Ahmed briefs me, was sixteen when he was shot to death three days ago while throwing stones outside one of the other Observation Posts. He died a hero's death, in the thick of battle, in the midst of driving the invaders from his country using the only weapon available. His father is a gray-haired, bearded man wearing a neat *jalabeeya* and a thin, embroidered *taghiya*, or skullcap. Next to a poster of his son, he sets his jaw, raises both hands in a "V" sign—for victory—and asks me to take a picture.

We are invited to visit his mother at the women's house. The *shabab* have been visiting her over the past two days, each saying, "Now we are all your sons. You have many sons." This helps some, Ahmed explains.

The women are in the family home. It is a small, dim place with dark walls, set near the abandoned railroad tracks. Three men of the family lead us through a tiny, cluttered foyer to the central room. Fifteen-odd women sit cross-legged on the thin foam mats so common in camp homes, each wearing identical black *hijab*, the kind worn for mourning. The men and the women exchange no words except "Peace be upon you."

One of my escorts indicates I may take pictures. I hold up my camera for the women to see, and tilt my head in an unspoken request for permission from them. No glances or nods; a few women slip their *hijab* over their faces. The man prods me. "It's okay," he says. I am profoundly uncomfortable. The light is low; I kneel outside the circle of women and make a half-dozen photos. I don't know if by doing this I am honoring her son or intruding on the women's ritual. If I ask the men later, they will of course tell me it is the former; how will I ever know?

We return to the men's house. Two young men are making rounds with long-spouted pots, pouring the unsweetened coffee used at ceremonies of marriage and death. A bowl of fresh dates circulates, too, and the pits are discreetly tossed underneath the chairs. In the lower room I spot Rafat Al Najjar, a

Beit shaheed: *the mother with friends and relatives of the martyr,*
March 23, 1993.

PFLP leader with nearly seventeen years of prison under his
belt, who was nearly expelled by Israel last summer, and who is
one of Mohammed's most notable relatives. I greet him and sit
next to him.

He tells me he can speak officially, as a member of his party.
Since the expulsions of December 17, he says, "Our position is
that the *intifada* must be stepped up in all respects." He points
to the posters of the martyr Salaam on the wall. "And this is
the present for the feast to the Palestinian people from Uncle
Sam."

I ask about the attacks on Israeli settlers and civilians.

"The policy is not to allow Israelis to feel safe in the Gaza
Strip or anywhere. Know that the settlers here are like another
division of the army. They all carry guns. They fight and shoot
us. They steal our land. Why shouldn't we fight them?

"And the killing here is not just by guns and the army," he
continues. "It is also economic. What would you do if someone took your food away from you and your family?"

On the third, final day of the feast, I walk over to Ahmed's house. Mohammed is working his last double shift, but none of the anticipated violence has materialized. It has, mercifully, been a quiet three days.

I find Ahmed, whom I now consider my best friend in the camp after Mohammed, standing in the rutted street near his family's house at the edge of the camp. He is walking slowly and seems truly depressed. We go back to his neat, icy blue living room lined with mats and the single desk he uses for his studies. He lies on his back, a pillow propped under his head. "As you can see," he begins, "I did not make celebration for this feast. I don't have any reason." He pauses.

I remember yesterday he mentioned that last night was the anniversary of the martyrdom of a good friend and neighbor. That, added to Salaam's martyrdom, Jihad's martyrdom, the mass shootings the week before—the grief surpasses anything I can link to my own life. All I can do is sit, and I listen to him.

"Have you thought more about Sudan these days?" I ask. He had received an offer a few weeks ago to attend a university in Khartoum, which he sees as his only way out of Gaza. Compared to Gaza, he had said, Sudan seems just fine.

"Yes," he says, "but how can I concentrate on any kind of work here for the university when there are confrontations and shooting every day?" Another long silence breaks his talk. "You know, sometimes, I don't think there is anything our people can do. What can we do? Israel, our enemy, is much too strong. The United States, the Security Council, they have all, everything in their hands. Most of our people, they are living like this, like us," he says, motioning to the block walls, the corrugated roof-ceiling, the scant furniture. "In Jabalia, Shaati, Bureij, Rafah, Maghazi, Shaboura, Lebanon, Jordan, West Bank—in every camp they are like this. I think that this is not even a life here. I, for me, I want to live. I think that I have to go out of this place. I tell you this is what I think sometimes, and I do not say this much to people. Nobody likes to hear this. You know why I like PFLP? The real reason?"

I shake my head.

"They have only a little money. They are the poor among the parties of ours. You know I don't like anyone who has a lot of money. I don't know why, I am just this way. I want more equality with money, let everyone be the same." He looks at me and a sardonic smile edges up slowly from his mouth. "I think in English this is what you would call a 'Romantic,' right?"

"You sound like an honest socialist," I reply. "Don't put down your ideals."

We sit a while longer. I sense his mind churning. We walk the mile to Mohammed's, speaking infrequently. Near the door he slips away, for the first time not making an arrangement to meet again. I fear only one thing: no matter how much we like each other, our circumstances may at some point prove unbridgeable. Me with cameras, passport, university research grant, wife and, above all, hopes; him with a scholarship to Sudan of all places, a political prison record, the prospect of an arranged marriage and the millstone of el wadd'a, the situation, slung about his neck every day of his twenty-third year in Khan Yunis Camp.

Although Ramadan has ended, the evening curfew has not, as everyone expected, reverted to 7:00 P.M. It is holding at 9:00. Mohammed seems flush with life tonight: an easy day at work, warm weather, a full day of food and tea and cigarettes seems to be doing him good. His mood is medicinal to me after the past four days. All too close to curfew he convinces me to come with him to visit another friend, old Abu Ziad.

We amble down his dark street, shaking hands with men sitting on the stoops. At the corner, we ascend a raw concrete stairway to a second floor of equally naked concrete, except for a few mats. It feels like a construction site more than a house.

Abu Ziad is nearly seventy. He moves trunk-like legs slowly, letting out a pained breath as he sits but still sending out a smile that furrows deep contours into his cheeks. He sits very close so he can see me through his eyes, milky with cataracts.

His wife, who seems younger, sits across the room from us after bringing a tray piled with date-filled pastries and tea.

After brief formalities, Abu Ziad begins speaking metaphorically, in a mixture of Arabic-for-the-foreigner and a ponderously slow English he picked up long ago as a driver for the British army, during the Mandate days, before Israel.

"It is like everywhere now," he says solemnly, "between all people there are walls just like these." He glances up, around at the mortared blocks rising above our heads. "We have to break them down to see! So it is good that you are here. Welcome."

I thank him and decide to pursue his symbolism. "Abu Ziad, the walls are very high between people in my country, in my government, and the people here." With this I strike that level of openness between men that back home would feel sentimental and sappy, but here every word is sincere. It is in moments like this I find myself perfectly content and never wanting to leave Gaza.

Abu Ziad marches a reply out word by word. "If you could teach my children, and I could then teach your children, this would destroy all the walls that are between the people."

I look at him, nod, and put one of his hands in mine. We sit quietly and savor the thought.

"Are you married?" he pops, his tone shifting to informal.

Oh no. Not again, I think to myself.

"Yes," I reply wearily, "and we don't have children. Next year, *insha'allah*." I add this in hopes of preempting an inevitable course of interrogatory.

"No children? Why not?" he says with perfectly timed indignation. "Is your wife, is she pregnant?"

"No!" I say, smiling now. "But next year, *insha'allah*!" Mohammed is giggling.

"Why not *now*?" Abu Ziad presses with a mischievous glint.

"Because I'm here and she's in America! She better not be!"

At this, he shudders, and his belly laugh sets off a coughing fit, which he salves by firing up another cigarette.

It's almost curfew.

CHAPTER 11

VOICES FROM CANADA CAMP

When I return to Mohammed's house following three days of writing in Rimal, it is March 29. He's earned a few extra vacation days for the overtime he worked during the feast, he tells me. Not only that, he says, as if hiding a present behind his back, he has at last arranged up to a dozen photo interviews in Canada Camp.

Not that our prospects for success feel more than slight. In the television room, Mohammed's mother is furrow-browed over our plan. "Why are you going to *Rafah*?" she inquires, speaking the name with more than a touch of revulsion. Even people in Khan Yunis, I have noticed, often look down on Rafah as dirtier, poorer, more violent and even "underdeveloped" compared to the rest of the Strip. Now, for the first time in my presence, she is critical of her son. She has her reasons: this morning soldiers prowled Khan Yunis and scared the kids back home on their way to school. Yesterday, Rafah was under curfew yet again while the army, ignoring the diplomatic immunity granted to UNRWA operations and property, took over an UNRWA school in Shaboura Camp for the day. Before dawn, the army trucked in computers and clerks and then rousted several thousand men out of their homes to check official records against faces in the army's campaign to ferret out "wanted men," known activists in any of the several factions. Mohammed and his RAO hung about the illegal operation for several hours and reported one sight with astonishment.

"Would you believe the soldiers were bringing tea and bread to the men as they waited, the detained ones?! And not beating them! They were actually treating them like human beings!" Although the use of the school is being protested through official channels, Mohammed is not one to bear a grudge. This memory is now filed away with the precious others he keeps concerning times Israeli soldiers have acted with restraint or compassion. Like the time the house-to-house search patrol found an *intifada* leaflet in Mohammed's bathroom wastebasket in 1989 and the commander let him off with a stern—but not abusive—reprimand. Possession of a leaflet at the time was punishable by six months "administrative detention," meaning no formal charges but prison with its beatings, interrogations and various other forms of torture. That Mohammed polishes these anecdotes with frequent tellings I consider an admirable effort in his struggle to keep his enemy human. Yesterday, he says, finishing his story, the army vacated the school in the night, and today it is open, no more curfew. But up north, he adds, the radio news said Erez checkpoint into Israel is shut down yet again and rumor is this time it will be for good.

What really worries Mohammed's mother, however, is that tomorrow is Land Day. On March 30, 1976, near Nazareth, six Palestinians were killed and seventy injured when they nonviolently tried to blockade an Israeli land theft operation. The incident became a national symbol and a day of protest—now often violent—against the ongoing, acre-by-acre Israeli whittling away of Palestinian lands. Today, the government of Israel and private Israeli citizens claim legal ownership and exert de facto control over nearly one-third of the Gaza Strip, and more than half the West Bank. Mohammed's mother expects nothing but trouble. But, Mohammed argues, now is our only chance: my funds run out in two weeks, and Mohammed has the rare days off. We go.

We ride to Canada Camp Palestine again via the single-lane dirt "Block J Beltway," inside of which more than 1,000 people are enduring—unbelievably—their twenty-seventh day of round-the-clock punitive curfew following the March 2 killing of the Israeli gas company accountant. UNRWA is still going from house to house in Block J delivering emergency rations.

A repatriated family arrives at their new home in Tel el Sultan from Canada Camp Egypt in the summer of 1992. The window broke in transit.

Canada Camp looks the same as ever: the reinforcing steel bars scraping at blue sky from roofs and the treeless, littered sand give it that forsaken feeling. But this has ceased to be exotic or unusual. It's become just where we work, when we can.

Old Abd El Rahman the barber is sitting with Abu Ahmed outside the two-chair barbershop. They are in the shade. The day is already a warning of summer's cruel blaze. They wave and call to us as our Peugeot taxi sputters away, leaving the street silent except for our voices. Their teapot is empty. Abd El Rahman insists on refilling it as he pumps Mohammed's hand as if Mohammed were the prodigal son himself. Mohammed declines the tea using an elaborate string of unusually polite phrases.

Across the road, a bulldozer is levelling open sand beyond the camp. It's for a soccer field, Abu Ahmed explains. The *shabab*, he says, went door to door in between curfews last week asking ten shekels from each house. With the proceeds, they hired the bulldozer from the municipality. It's the first positive sign of change in the camp I've noticed.

Our first interview is a group affair. With a dozen mostly young men from several families, we sit about a garage packed with mattresses, door frames, windows, old and new furniture, tools, scrap lumber and a mothballed Mercedes taxi. Only after they are satisfied with our intentions do they agree to talk. My questions are often answered by several people at once, and Mohammed assembles the comments into a single, translated response. I still find the basics of their repatriation process murky, so I begin by asking about the practical side of their move from Canada Camp, Egypt, to Canada Camp, Palestine.

"We started building maybe in October of '91," begins one, "about eight months ahead of our move, as soon as we had our check [for $12,000 from the PLO via Egypt]. Someone from the Housing Department came and inspected at times, checking the style of the house, you know, regulations. He said we had to plaster the outside and put stucco on before he'd call it finished. Only the outside was important to the government, to show in the media a comparison between the houses here and the poor-looking ones we left in Canada Camp Egypt."

On moving day from Canada Camp Egypt, this family— which asked not be named—spent the equivalent of $2,000 to hire trucks and workers, one set on each side of the border. I pull out several photos of a move I witnessed briefly last summer. I point to the possessions piled willy-nilly in the truck. How does it come to look this way, I ask.

"It's complicated," I hear. "Like the family in your picture, the Egyptians didn't allow us to unload for customs by ourselves, even though we had lots of boxes of glass things. They threw the boxes from the truck even though they knew what was in them."

"What did you do?"

"What could we do? If we moved to stop them we would have been arrested."

He continues, explaining that this actually happens to only one or two families out of each group of thirty-five. Upon reaching the Israeli side, however, loading and unloading for customs is up to the family itself. But there, "the police tell us to hurry, hurry, move faster and so we end up breaking things that way, too. For us when we moved we had only fifteen to thirty minutes to reload each truck, and they said anything we didn't get back on in time they would confiscate."

"What are the tasks of men and women that day?" I ask.

"The women organize and prepare all the household goods. The men are interested in finishing the building, getting the trucks. Building materials are all cheaper in Egypt, especially the finished products like windows and doors and furniture. And then the whole community always helps in the first loading and the last unloading, here."

"You know, we were forced to build these kinds of nice-looking concrete houses," says another. "It's a way to erase what the government calls their 'refugee problem.'" It accomplishes three things for the government, he says: First, the place no longer looks like what outsiders will think of as a "refugee camp." Second, control over housing plot assignment can be used to break up blocs based on kinship, political faction and village of origin. Finally, the debt families incur in construction creates a disincentive to activism.

"We get loans only from family and friends. We've spent everything. Now, I'm not crazy enough to involve myself in factions that might lead to [the army] demolishing my house. If it were an asbestos-roofed one, like the poor ones, maybe I could accept its being demolished, but not this one!"

"And the government insisted on reinforced concrete slab construction also because it allows the houses to go higher," says another, "reducing the land they need to give each Palestinian family. This policy allows more families to occupy the same 200 meters. But look at how they build in the settlements! One house, one family, lots of land everywhere. You know today is Land Day?"

I nod and shift into a more personal arena. "So what is it like, psychologically, to come here from Egypt and be with other men who have been through the *intifada* when you haven't?"

"The main thing you have to avoid here is to talk or be involved in politics, just like in Egypt," Mohammed translates. "We know the Egyptians don't want to be bad, but they are under pressure from Camp David. Egypt and Israel accepted a common but unspoken goal with that treaty, and that was to keep Palestinians from doing anything against Israel from anywhere, including Canada Camp Egypt. So the Egyptian government has to act the way it does. But it's totally different here psychologically. It was actually less stressful back there."

"What more can you say about how it feels to come home to the occupation?"

"We suffer depression a lot," says one at once. Four others concur by nodding. "We've come, like, from a kind of freedom to a prison. All the young men suffer. Someday we might have to build an insane asylum here just for the *shabab*! You can't go anywhere, there's curfew every other day, Erez is closed so you can't work in Israel, you don't ever feel safe anywhere, so what do we do? We are constantly afraid of being arrested or beaten or exposed to shooting. Constantly."

"So what do you do when you feel this?"

"Everyone becomes nervous, agitated, angry. We have fights at home, in the streets. And many of us don't have money to get married even, you know? That makes it worse."

Another asks, "So what about you? Have you gotten depressed here yet?" A dozen pairs of eyes turn to me.

"Of course," I say, shrugging, "but I come and go as I please. I have another life I can leave and go home to. If I couldn't do this, believe me, I'd be right there helping you build the Canada Camp insane asylum."

Land Day passes without a curfew-inducing incident anywhere in the southern Strip, but the day after, a general strike protesting what is now officially the permanent closure of the border with Israel keeps everyone at home. For our purposes, ironically, nothing could be better than a general strike. Our requests for interviews are received warmly now, as if word has gotten around that we are to be trusted. Talk is lively, fueled again by the high-octane tea that was denied during Ramadan. At last we begin to use photographs as our questions.[1] The comments on the images, we hope, will illuminate life in Canada Camp from the point of view of those who live there as purely as we can muster. We once thought of asking people to make the photographs themselves, but then rejected this as too dangerous.

Mohammed sets up, in a spontaneous kind of way, interviews with five men and four women of varying ages. As we begin each session, the person hears from Mohammed that we hope to put these comments into a book, so they know they are speaking publicly. He assures them real names will not be used. He patiently explains his family lineage, our friendship, my funding sources and whatever else the person requires to feel safe in speaking. Each person then looks over eighty-three photographs Mohammed and I assembled from the nearly eighty rolls of film I've shot so far. Each person chooses twelve photos and then arranges them in their own order from their most important image on down. At that point, Mohammed asks each person to talk about the pictures one by one, using whatever words feel appropriate.

In living rooms, yards and shops, from morning until long after curfew, we listen and prompt and write, noting every detail, including our own questions. As one interview follows on another, it feels to me a sea at last has parted before us. Mohammed assures me our good fortune is not due to luck, but to all our prior visits, and to the willingness of people to take risks to make themselves heard.

Only months later, through correspondence, will we edit what becomes two notebooks of transcripts. From our records of each person's ordering of his or her twelve pictures, we will assemble a composite sequence, allowing us to publish the photos, with the comments, in a sequence dictated by the group's idea of what is significant rather than our own. We will have to edit to less than one-fourth the original length, but in doing so, we agree to uphold the spirit of the longer version as faithfully as possible.

The most frequently chosen and highly ranked photo came as a surprise. Six respondents placed it at or near the top of their stack. As with the other photographs presented here, not all responses are included, and others are edited.

Aysha, forty-two, a teacher: "This picture was taken in Canada Camp Egypt. It shows the mosque of Canada Camp

and the destroyed houses, which were destroyed [by the people in the camp] to prevent Egyptians from moving in when we left. There is a man who used to be good in the background. There, see? He has a psychological depression, and he has become crazy. He was a contractor, and very strong. He married two wives, and one left him. When we were in Canada Camp, in Egypt, we were living under asbestos sheets but we were happier than we are now."

Ayman, twenty-four, a student: "This picture shows where I lived for thirteen or maybe fifteen years. And suddenly I see for the first time that place is demolished. You know there is a poem that says that your longing for home is always strongest for your first home, everywhere you go. And for me, the first place I grew up in was Canada Camp. I miss that mosque so much. That was where I started learning to pray. And near to it is the playground. Many times I played in it. I miss those times."

Yusef, thirty, an unemployed nurse: "My house was just fifty or seventy meters away from here along the mosque road. The destroyed house I can see used to be my neighbor. And I don't know how to describe coming from that place to this place where I can't be familiar with the life anymore. It takes a lot of time, at least four or five years to be familiar with the situation in Gaza Strip. We used to live in a closed area in Canada Camp Egypt. You see, each person knew the others and we shared each type of, what, of occasion. But here in Rafah Palestine we are dealing with a new people although they are relatives to us. But we feel this is still something strange."

The second photo, however, was no surprise at all *(see next page)*.

Adil, thirty-eight, a construction laborer: "This picture is about the border that was fixed in 1982, that separated Rafah into two parts. This began the suffering of our people."

Ayman: "Even the Egyptians find that moments like this are still too big a gift to give to Palestinians, so they have built that wall. Only your head can be shown."

"How do you feel when you go there?"

"I talk to my friends there, you see, and we remember the days we spent together before I came here. I hate going there. I feel sick there."

Yusef: "This picture reminds me that my sister calls us via the border. I don't know what else to say. It cannot be explained how a family comes to be divided and to talk along the border like this. The picture must explain itself. It shows how Palestinian life either inside Palestine or outside— *khalass*," he says, "finished."

Rula, nineteen, a college student: "All the people who see this leave weeping. You can't feel any freedom talking there, as you sense that you are watched all the time. While I go to see my

friends, I feel I am with them for a while. But after that it's so bad a feeling. I feel that they are really far away after that."

Aysha: "The most sad thing I've seen at the border was one of the youths living here in Rafah [Palestine], when his mother died in Canada Camp Egypt, he couldn't get permission to visit. So he asked the funeral procession to pass by the fence. I saw him."

Ayman: "This is a passport for people who haven't a home. In any airport in the world, when the passport officer sees this, he will say, 'Okay, sit down over there.' It carries no respect."

Rula: "Up to now, there is no Palestinian with his own passport. From my childhood I've heard the word 'refugee' with the word 'Palestinian.' Up to now we don't have anything our own."

Ahmed, sixteen, a secondary school student: "The word passport I've seen all my life. . . . The Gulf [Arab] country citizens and the foreigners, they can pass into any country with their passports. But with ours it is impossible."

Hashim, fifty-two, a civil servant: "Now we've come to our *mujaheddin,* our strugglers. This is a look at our masked men. They are sacrificing of themselves and their souls, even though they are in danger every minute. [Israeli army military orders permit soldiers to shoot masked men on sight.] Despite their understanding of this danger, they sacrifice. This picture lets hope rise and be renewed in our souls. . . . Most of these men are civilized, educated men and most of them are university graduates. They are our hope. We have a poem by one of our famous poets, Abdel-Rahim Mahmoud. It's about the martyrs. 'I'll hold my soul in my palm / And hurl it into hell / To get one of two things / Either a good life to please my friends / Or a death to displease my enemies.' These people absolutely are not killers at heart. They are not terrorists, because they seek only to live as well as the other people and to take their place on the land and under the sun. It's a very human behavior that if you can't resolve a problem with those who take away your rights, you'll try to force them by your own hand. You yourself, in America, if you feel any government takes your rights,

you'll hope all of the people and all of the country that does this will be burned and will go to hell. It's only human."

Mouna, twelve, a middle-school student: "I'm not afraid of the masked men. I stand when they are coming, to watch them. If the soldiers come and the masked men see them, I'll run away. But if the masked people don't see the soldiers, I'll yell to warn them before I run. If the soldiers want to catch them, I'll throw stones with the other kids to let them get away. These kids are waiting around, watching for soldiers. The cars here are stopping, to make a kind of barrier to protect them."

Hashim: "This reminds me of another poem, where a daughter is speaking to her father. 'Leila came to her father / With pain in her eyes / Asking why are we abandoned my father? / Haven't we friends and loved ones all over the world?'"

Rula: "This is Khan Yunis, a demolished house. The soldiers have demolished many houses without just cause. This child seems very sad. In his eyes he wants to kill the soldiers. He feels hate. I feel the suffering here—like we are victims without reason. If you hear about it only, you cannot feel it as you do when you actually see it. I wonder how the person who owns this house feels. He sees all his life black. Everything beside him is black. I feel a challenge, an insistence in the eyes of these children to continue the resistance, to continue the way of *intifada*."

Ahmed: "We put all our life into building our houses, and they take two minutes to destroy them. . . . These houses cost a

lot of money and the people can't save again to reconstruct it. . . . If I see any family's house demolished, and I see the people on the street, I feel as if it is my home they have destroyed."

Yusef: "This is the market in Canada [Camp, Egypt,] that my mother and my wife used to bring all our needs from. I know most of the people who sell vegetables and meat over there. I feel now like I'm sitting, I'm walking in this market again. This is a very clear picture. I know these people, selling onion, potato, cucumber—and at cheaper Egyptian prices!"

Adil: "When the border came, we didn't have a market, so they opened it in the middle of the school street. There was harassment from the Egyptian government against our merchants. If anybody was selling anything at more than the stan-

dard price [the one set by the Egyptian government] they would put him in jail in special cells, beat him, and make him pay 300 pounds. I remember one problem. One man, Abu Nasser, was selling salt. And one time he sold his salt for one-tenth of an Egyptian pound, ten piasters, more than the government price. Some of the informers came to him, tied his hands, beat him and slapped him in the street and took him to the police station. He had no money to pay and no one to help him. They put him in an isolated cell, a bad and miserable one, at the police station in Rafah [Egypt]. In the end we took up a collection in the camp for nearly all the 300-pound fine, and they released him."

"When was this?"

"About five years ago, maybe in '87 or '88."

"Was this common?"

"From time to time. Another man, Abu Jaber, was selling oil. They broke his hand and burned his face with acid in the

Abu Za'bal prison in east Cairo. He was there ten months, and the family paid nearly 30,000 pounds to lawyers, for food, transport and other things."

"What did they accuse him of?"

"At first they accused him of selling stolen oil from UNRWA, but he was really just selling it secondhand. They also accused him of insulting and resisting the soldiers and intelligence men. When they came to arrest him, people began to throw stones. It changed from a commercial problem to a political problem. He and his wife are psychological cases because of this now. He sits alone in or out of his home, hardly breathing with depression."

Aysha: "This is Jerusalem, the capital of Palestine. All the eyes of the children are looking forward to the day they liberate it

from the Israeli Jews. Every house in Gaza Strip has this [kind of] picture, because Jerusalem is so precious to us. These children see it in pictures only. But they hope."

Rula: "The kids all over the world in this age have much luxury and leisure time, but ours, they are born to hear about martyrs, prisoners, injuries, the death of their father or brother. If we compare kids in Canada Camp [Egypt] and kids here, we find many differences between them. In Canada Camp a child can play and run and watch TV, but here the child everywhere sees a soldier and a curfew and doesn't enjoy life."

Rula: "This speaks about the prisons under occupation. I wish I could live near it and visit every week to see my uncle, who is like a brother to me, who is here. You see the soldiers surrounding them. All the time when I go there I ask him to come out with me, but of course he can't . . . At visiting time, [the prisoners]

are so anxious to see their families. It's a hard time. In this small room [she points to the white block building] you couldn't imagine—there are twenty prisoners with their families, four visitors to each. Nearly 100 people in that tiny room. You can't see and talk easily as everyone wants to talk and they are shouting through the two layers of fencing in the house. As a prisoner, if you want to talk you have to crouch as the window is at knee height. The families are crying and crying for more time with their sons because the visits are only a few minutes."

"Is it like this for you when you go there?"

"Yes. You know, wherever you go in Palestine you see a fence somewhere, surrounding someone."

Hashim: "The kids outside of our country, they are no better than our kids. We have intelligent and good kids. They try to survive despite the situation. Most kids here have bad situations—their father is killed, injured, sick, or jobless. But they

keep trying to find their way despite the difficulties they face. Kids from anywhere else in the world, if they come to live under these bad conditions, I am sure they couldn't manage so well. Ours are so intelligent and smart in their education, even though there isn't much electricity or water. It's the life in our camps. This picture here is self-explanatory. You feel the presence of many principles of land and family. She is holding her brother in one hand and the beans in the other. You can see in her eyes the hope of the alleviation of her poverty, because she is smiling. Despite the poverty, the bitterness, the wounded hearts, there is one day I am positive they are going to take their rights to live as human beings, just like people in other countries. Despite all, we must stand with our heads high."

Rula: "You know, we were able to express ourselves back there [in Canada Camp Egypt]. But it wasn't easy to do this. Inside our classrooms, at the secondary school, all the teachers are Egyptian, and sometimes they would insult the PLO or our leaders. We couldn't do anything out of fear for our families."

"What were you afraid of?"

"The intelligence would take you at two or three in the night to El Arish [fifty miles away]. Maybe also, the teachers, after they provoked us, maybe they don't let you pass the class.

"You know, during the *intifada* there were celebrations [on the Gaza Strip side of the border], and we couldn't join in. Especially at these times the [Egyptian] intelligence people would come and strictly observe us. . . . One time there was a celebration for the *intifada* anyway and immediately we saw four [Egyptian] soldier trucks come right into the school. All the intelligence people surrounded the school, and one of the high ranking officers went inside to prevent any celebration. It was the first anniversary of the declaration of the State of Palestine. This was in November '89. Another time they shot tear gas because some youths threw stones on the Israelis from the fence. The Egyptian soldiers shot tear gas at us! On one of the anniversaries of the *intifada*! One other time there was like a confrontation against the Israelis in Rafah, and the youths in Canada tried to support it. The [Egyptian] officers began throwing stones at our youths, and the next night all of the youths were arrested. Girls only had their names registered, maybe forty or fifty of them. Then from the beginning of the

intifada many youths were deported [from Canada Camp]. I have two cousins deported recently to Libya after a year in an Egyptian jail."

Ayman: "Now you ask if there is anything else you should be taking pictures of. The only thing that is missing is to show the deportees' families. My cousin is one, in Libya. Most are there in Libya, but some in Sudan also. I know more than 100 *shabab* were deported from Canada Camp. For political reasons. No one likes to talk about it. Even now, I would prefer not to. But they are there. I know you can't really take their pictures, but you know for us, we think about them so much."

Note

1. We hardly came to this idea on our own. Visual social science has long used "photo elicitation" as a means of creating a nonthreatening interview environment that encourages those who are photographed by outsiders to explain the images in their own terms. See, for example, John Collier, Jr., and Malcolm Collier, *Visual Anthropology: Photography as a Research Method* (Albuquerque: University of New Mexico Press, 1986); as well as academic journals *Visual Sociology, Qualitative Sociology* and *Visual Anthropology.*

Chapter 12
Closure

In the overcast of an early April dawn, a ghost-town calm has settled on Erez checkpoint, normally as crowded as a tollbooth in rush hour. Plastic bags tumble among empty rows of stalls that used to offer fruit, vegetables, falafel and bread to the workers who directly supported more than one-third of all Gaza Strip families, and whose purchasing power supported thousands more. I ride to Jerusalem with an Italian UNRWA official on personal business: no more taxis. Like curfews, the March 29 sealing of the Israeli borders with the Gaza Strip and West Bank applies only to Palestinians of those areas. The few soldiers on duty wave us past. In East Jerusalem, I walk unimpeded along narrow sidewalks that should be impassable with shoppers.

Closure is in its tenth day now. Gazans are confined within the Strip. West Bankers keep to either north or south of Jerusalem. East Jerusalem residents cannot leave their section of the annexed city, although Jewish settlers living there can come and go at will. UNRWA calculates income from the lost wages among Gazan workers alone at $5.25 million already; tomorrow, this will rise by another day's total of $750,000. Unemployment has topped 50 percent from its "normal" 35 to 40 percent, all this in the Strip, where per capita annual income is about $850. Businesses inside the Strip, unable now to import essential materials, are choked off, too. After twenty-six years of strategically nurturing a dependent economy in the West Bank and Gaza Strip, closure is somewhere between divorce and a severing of an umbilical cord. The *Jerusalem Post* this morning quotes Prime Minister Rabin: "We must see to it that Palestinians do not swarm among us." A subsequent article confirms "swarm" was indeed an accurate English translation from Hebrew.

150

For two days, I go over our interviews and process more photographs in East Jerusalem. Easter weekend begins tomorrow, and it won't be very crowded this year. Several thousand Palestinian Christians from the West Bank will not be allowed past the roadblocks north and south of Jerusalem. Thursday evening I phone Mohammed. He tells me Khan Yunis is under curfew yet again because the army is confiscating two acres just out of town for a new army post. "They keep the whole town and camp in our houses just because they do not want resistance," he says.

Friday morning I buy a ticket at the Israeli West Jerusalem bus station for a ninety-minute ride to Ashdod, or, in Arabic, Isdud. I want to see this coastal city three out of four of the families in Canada Camp call their real home, the place where their ancient roots lie buried yet thick, resilient and perhaps still fecund after a half century of dispossession. In Canada Camp, I have asked several times what I might find remaining here of pre-1948 life. Not much, I heard: a cafe, maybe; a few houses scattered in a few old farms, maybe; a saint's tomb and a ruined mosque on the outskirts; and a huge, shady tree. This tree was the only thing everyone agreed upon. Everything else, I was told, is gone, erased from the land and official memory along with the other 416 Palestinian villages inside Israel destroyed since 1948. The exact locations of even these traces were uncertain from person to person, as if the old, material Isdud is disappearing even in memory, leaving only nostalgia to fill the vacuum.

But no one spoke as expansively about Isdud as sixty-three-year-old Abu Yasser. Like everyone else, his ancestors were Philistines who, in about 1200 B.C., carved out a home on the coastal plains among Egyptians to the west, Phoenicians to the north, and the Israelites—themselves newly arrived from slavery along the Nile—to the northeast. Abu Yasser's people farmed that fertile and strategic land continuously as empires rose and fell over three thousand years.

"The land in Isdud is like nothing you've seen anywhere else," he told me. "There are oranges, figs, almonds, cabbages as big as this!" He held his arms out to nearly full spread, a gesture more suited to a cow than a cabbage.

"No!" I replied playfully, "cabbages don't get that big!"

"Yes! Yes, in Isdud they do! And watermelons—I used to see them there as big as fifty-eight kilos! Isdud is better than anywhere!" He went on like this for some time, eyes wide with sincerity. He was thirteen when the Israeli army forced his family to flee the farm he was due to inherit.

But the tree, he had said, the big tree, "this is the closest to my heart." It's a *jumaiz* tree, a sycamore, enormous and generous of shade, laden with tiny fruit all year round in seven cycles, dwarfing every other tree in town, a landmark for generations rising at the head of the main street parallel to the sea, with a big drinking fountain next to it and benches underneath. "Just look there for the biggest tree, one so big even the Israelis will know it well," he instructed me.

The bus is half full with young Israelis in military fatigues, teenagers mostly, attractive young men and women each slinging a duffel bag and an M-16. They look so clean, so strong and disciplined and well-schooled. Their teeth and skin are good, not like Gazans, who suffer at early ages from the drinking water with twenty-five times normal salinity and over-fluoridation that browns the teeth, from exposure and poverty and stress of insecurity that weathers a face quickly. I want to talk to these kids, ask where they are going and what they are doing, but I hesitate: if they reciprocate and ask what I'm up to, I won't know what to say, or just how to say it. It is as if the Gaza-Israel border is closed today in my own mind, too. I sit alone.

On first sight, Ashdod is a pristine town, green and suburban in its sprawl. Apartment blocks stack a dozen stories each up from watered lawns against twin blues of sky and Mediterranean. Here is everything Gaza isn't, an inverted world, a kind of parallel universe of plenty. There are stoplights here, and painted crosswalks for pedestrians. Flower

boxes decorate the median on the paved main street that has
no potholes. Drivers don't have to honk. Cafes spill plastic
chairs and tables onto wide, well-swept sidewalks every few
hundred yards. A public phone is always within sight, and—I
check a few out—they work. No garbage. No horse or donkey
carts. No puddles of dark, smelly muck.

But nor is there a tree fitting the descriptions I carry. There
are lots of trees, but every one looks young and decorous. The
historical center of Isdud was about a mile from here, but still,
I was assured that the tree was here, as before 1948 it lay on
the edge of town. I stop passersby who speak English; none
know any landmark sycamore predating their country's founding. In the office of the national bus company's tourism
agency, wallpapered with bright posters hawking guided trips
to Masada, Acre, Jerusalem, the Negev and the Galilee, two
women shrug. I begin fearing the tree may have been cut
down. I amble back toward the head of the main street one
more time.

Here I register an old railroad station converted into a center for immigration bearing a sign in Hebrew, English and
Russian. More buildings, new shops and small offices and
walkup apartments; in a park, paved walking paths are lined
with benches and lots of little, leafy trees, not one oversize or
grandly welcoming. Through a passageway under an office
building, I spot the white chairs of a cafe that appears protected
from what is becoming a hot Mediterranean sun. Coffee beck-
ons. Maybe someone in there will know something. Maybe
someone will know when it was cut down, and why.

I traverse a compact plaza. A small fountain muffles four
lanes of traffic with a simple but delicate plume. The cafe is
one of perhaps a dozen shops, part of a small, squarish shopping arcade. Gray offices of no architectural inspiration rise on
two sides, creating a kind of half cube of space. In the middle,
with sagging branches approaching each of the atrium's four
sides, is a tree. But it is not so big, not really. I stop and exam-
ine it anyway, recalling Abu Yasser's six-foot, two-hundred-
pound cabbage. I wonder.

My question must seem odd to the two heavily made-up young women working the cafe. "Well," says the one who speaks English, "I think it is not like any other tree here, but it's not like special or anything." And no—they consult each other—they've never seen any fruit on it. Don't know what kind it is, either. I can't find anyone who can translate "sycamore" into Hebrew.

I look it over some more. That fountain I passed—that could have been a public tap once. And this tree does outsize everything else I've seen, though not by much. It is, after all, at the top of the main street, more or less. As I circle it, I gradually come to think that yes, this probably is the tree after all. But I feel let down. It projects only the most modest dignity, nothing like the regal bearing I'd anticipated. It looks tired, really, a sagging and lonely centerpiece of a humdrum shopping mall. Electric cords dangle from a few giant, knotty branches that start but a few feet off the ground, left over from a forgotten holiday. Leaves hang motionless, cut off from the sea breeze, gathering a film of dirt. It looks like a giant potted plant, domesticated, contained, and not very well-cared-for at that.

I forego coffee. I wonder if Abu Yasser really knows his tree is no longer the town's welcome sign atop his main street of memory? If this and a ruined building or two is all that's left of Isdud, I think, I don't want to show a picture of any of it to him, or to anyone in Canada Camp. Do I want him to learn through a photograph, during these days of closure—imprisonment, really—how his precious, remaining material link to the earth of his identity has been boxed in and impounded as graphically as every Palestinian soul in the Gaza Strip? Do I want to tell him fruit is no longer seen on it, that perhaps through incarceration and solitary confinement his tree has gone barren?

I wander only a little more, behind the arcade now. I can see the green roundness of the tree poking up over the one-story flat roof of the mall. I'm among pet stores, clothing stores and groceries and white-stripe parking lots filled with cars, all with yellow license plates and not one of them an aging white Peugeot 404. I buy an ice cream bar that begins melting in the sun. They were right, of course. There is no trace, except perhaps out on the outskirts of town, of an Isdud. What did I expect, I scold myself, historical markers? I reboard the Jerusalem bus feeling empty, as if I have just experienced Ashdod not only with my own senses, but with those eyes and hearts of each person I've sat with on the sands of Canada Camp, a whole crowd now, reaching, straining, held back by bullets and razor wire from the edge of the daily widening abyss separating desire and dreaming in Gaza from the unshared abundance of real-life Israel.

By the time I get back to the Old City in Jerusalem, the Good Friday procession is over. Television crews, photographers and pilgrim-tourists still hang about the stony Via Dolorosa, awaiting perhaps a straggler group of cross-bearing monks. I spot a news photographer I've met before. He's gripping a cellular phone in one hand and dangling a cigarette from the other. He courteously blows the smoke up over his head. Got sent to Sarajevo, he says, when I ask him what he's been shooting lately. I am several years his professional junior. He returns the question and I tell him.

"That's great," he says. "Gaza is definitely hot. Lots of people doing projects there now. Agencies sending people and stuff. Heavy stuff there." He drops a few names, big ones, power hitters on the global photojournalism circuit who have dropped in—"parachuted" is the industry term—for a day or a week just as a city news "shooter" drops in at a fire, tries to put on film some flames, some emotion. No, I haven't run into any of them. We chat, and secretly, disturbingly, I find myself envying them. Even though such "action" isn't the point of my mission, still, among photographers, assignments mean your work is in demand. Nobody's been calling me lately.

Our brief exchange depresses me for another reason. It's not him. I like him. It's how I myself change in such an encounter, unless I am careful, and today I am not. I don't want to talk about Gaza in a casual, desensitized, barroom kind of way, as if the place is a safari park for earning—or squandering—my photographer's living and the currency that comes with risking one's life with a camera. Something gets into our way of talking, at that moment. There is a protective layer that I don't sense in my talk with Mohammed or Ahmed or Rowhi or other men in Gaza, men who live *el wadd'a* day in and day out, men for whom "occupation" and "neo-colonialism" are not abstractions but living realities that affect themselves and their children. It is as if in my talk I leave no space for meaningful acknowledgment of what either of us has seen, him in Sarajevo, me in Gaza. He doesn't, either. There is no room for acknowledging the way witnessing something might change you. For real, unsentimental compassion. For what he really saw and felt in Sarajevo; what I've really seen and felt in Khan Yunis, in Canada Camp. What we know but we won't, can't, don't know how to say.

As we part I feel between worlds. I go back to Gaza.

From one of Gaza city's only public telephones, in the closet-like city post office, I put a call through to Khan Yunis.

"No, it is still curfew here today," Mohammed says with characteristically ironic cheer. "And such a strong one again. Even I don't believe it! Again the people with passes, like me, even we cannot go out. And they have brought in new soldiers from the Golani division, and they are being so bad. They were kicking a doctor here in Khan Yunis, I heard from one of my friends who called me. They want to prove to us they are stronger than us."

"So are you really as okay as you sound?"

"You know Dick, we have to cope in some way," he says. "For me it is to just stay here with the family and try to enjoy the time, do some reading if I can. For others, maybe it is not so easy, like Rafat. He is just watching television."

I promise I'll be down as soon as the curfew lifts.

The next morning I do laundry in Rimal, relax in a wicker chair, watch the sea and wait. It's Easter Sunday, the day when, in my tradition, the unshakable unity of life and death is celebrated. It is a day of hope, *amal.* It feels ironic. Maybe that's the point. Mid-morning the curfew is up, and, as often happens following a curfew, the road south is heavy with post-curfew traffic. The army jeeps crawl along at twenty mph, as they always do, keeping everything slower still. A new checkpoint delays us just outside Khan Yunis. They are checking hard. My Mercedes taxi is full of old men and women, which I had chosen on purpose, just in case there was something like this. It's young men they look for, the wanted ones, activists. I cram my camera bag out of sight and register the soldiers with peripheral vision only. On the left, six Palestinian men are facing a wall, hands above their heads, being frisked. We get a wave. Not so much adrenaline this time. Adaptation.

In Rafah, Block J has been at last released from its more than three weeks of twenty-four-hour curfew, too, leaving the main road to Tel el Sultan open again at last. In Canada Camp, Mohammed and I find another group of young men, most of whom we haven't met before. We sit on steps in the shade, out of the sun. I make some photographs, taking my permissions in nods and glances, and, as usual, no one wants even their first name used. Somebody complains about marriage, how with closure now none of the men can hope to save enough for a wedding. But I'm not in the mood for writing down more complaints. This might be our last interview here, and I have some questions that have come up since last week's sessions.

"What goes through your mind when you see someone like me, someone obviously foreign, probably a journalist? What's the first thing you think?" I ask.

"When I see a foreign journalist the first thing I think is they belong to the Shin Bet. They've used this cover many times," one says.

Shin Bet is Israeli domestic intelligence. The most notorious incident of an undercover unit disguising itself as journalists occurred when a "television crew" entered a market in

Beach Camp outside Gaza city in 1991 and assassinated, death-squad-style, its target activist, and then wounded roughly a dozen more people as the "crew" shot its way out.

"For me, all Westerners are the same, especially Americans, British and French. They all might be collaborators with Israel," says another lazily.

"What if I was a Jew from America and not a Christian? What would you say to me?" I ask.

"I'd say if you were a Jew, then you're behind all of the problems in the world, and please stop it."

No one adds anything. I'm getting used to hearing this.

"Have you ever had any good experiences with Jews?"

"Maybe once you run into this kind of thing, but a million other times they are so bad to us."

"Yes," says another, older man. "You know before the *intifada*, if a Jew wasn't a soldier, you could talk about lots of things. Before the border in 1982, I was working in the *kibbutzim*, farm work. They asked me to write an article about the Palestinian question since 1917, from my point of view. I wrote four pages, and they translated it into Hebrew. I also know some of them will spend a month in jail rather than serve in the military. You can find some like this."

After a time we are invited into a living room where a set of upholstered green armchairs appear to float in the middle. Only a tiny picture of the Dome of the Rock hangs high on one of the otherwise blank walls. There are eight of us, mostly the older ones from the steps outside. Still no introductions are made but mine: if I am going to take quotes, they want to remain anonymous. Real talk begins when tea appears, courtesy of our host's unseen mother.

"What do you do with your feelings of hate?" I ask, assuming by now that no one will bother to deny having them.

"There is no single word that can fully explain the hate," says one. "We've seen so many things. It makes hate something bigger than anything that can be explained."

"Imagine yourself in our position," says another, "harassed, killed, injured. What can you say? If you had to name these things at all, then maybe we could name them using just one word: 'occupation.'"

"But any word you use is never enough to completely explain the feeling," the first one emphasizes.

"We will forget the killing when they leave us," says another. They are taking careful turns speaking. "But we don't want to allow them to harm us until they do leave, and we don't really want to harm them. And we don't deny that we learned many things from them, and we taught them things, too."

"Such as?" I prompt.

"They are a democratic people inside. We've tried to learn that from them. And for us, we've built the whole Israeli state from our hands and our shoulders as workers in Israel. We don't say only they have a dark, or evil side. They have a light side, too, a good one. All the time," he adds, "we are living in hope, hoping to deal with each other with clean and pure hands."

"What do you think of the peace process now? Could it lead to that?" I feel like I am broaching a taboo subject, like asking about sex. Palestinians have refused to continue the bilateral Washington talks until Israel abides by UN Resolution 799 and allows the return of Muslim leaders expelled in December.

"We are optimistic to find a solution by the end of this year," says one.

"According to the Qur'an the occupation will be continued," says another, bitterly. "In the Qur'an it says where there are Jews there will be the destruction of homes."

Mohammed challenges him, "Where does it say this? Do you know the place? Where in the Qur'an?"

The man shakes his head, and looks down, embarrassed. "All we want from them is to leave," he replies, not looking up.

In Khan Yunis after dinner, more men, six of us, cram into a tiny television salvage shop, full of dusty flotsam of the early and middle electronic ages. First, *el wadd'a*, the situation: the group agrees there is not one but two new army encampments in villages near Khan Yunis. In the latest two-day curfew, the army felled eight houses, not by artillery but "only" by TNT. Three men from the Red Eagles armed faction were arrested in house-to-house searches.

I mention I went to Isdud. Eyes widen.

"I have the papers for my land in Isdud," says the shop owner, raising his chin, thin and stubbled, from his hand, elbow propped on a filthy shelf. "I have them in my house. And even if there is peace, or a state, I have got to tell my sons, 'Here, this is our land, and if you are stronger than I have been, then take it back, for it is ours.' We cannot deny our history. And Israel knows this very well. I've taken my children to see our land, and we even met the Jewish owner. He gave us some fruit from the trees, new trees. He was nice, not a bad man, but he said there was nothing he could do, it was all in the government's hands." His voice thickens with contempt.

"So even if there are two states," he declares, "I will still teach my children to say 'I am from Isdud.' This is our history."

And what Isdud will that be? I wonder silently, remembering Abu Yasser's vestigial old sycamore potted in the shopping mall.

I wake in the television room of Mohammed's house to the purr of the electric washing machine and the swish-slap of a broom on the tile floor. Drops of sun filter through the cracks in the corrugated roofing.

As I walk out to brush my teeth, Aysha and Suzanne are already rolling out the day's bread. The round loaves make a polka dot pattern on trays on the floor. I go up into the living room to write notes until Mohammed rises. We were up late, trying to keep my last night in his house from passing.

I've barely opened my notebook when Mohammed's mother slowly ascends the two steps into the room bearing in her hands a white *hijab*, the thin kind worn by the older women throughout Palestine, but nowhere as commonly as in the Gaza Strip. It is a gift.

"Is this okay?" she asks. "Is this a good one for Kathy?"

"Yes," I say softly, touching the simple, embroidered edge. I can see my fingers clearly through the light fabric. "It is very beautiful."

"And she can wear it like this," she adds, draping the cloth over her shoulders and wrapping it scarf-like around her neck. This lets me know she knows my wife will not wear it over her head as would a Muslim woman, and that this is fine. Her smile as she places it into my hands is all I see. "Now you must give her greetings from everyone here," she says in her Arabic simplified to my ability, "and tell her she has to come with you next time!"

I splutter something fractured but, I hope, sufficiently gracious. She smiles again and withdraws, back to the kitchen, leaving me standing with it draped over my hands and arms. It is so delicate I hardly detect weight, and its softness melts me like the touch of a priest's benediction on my head as a small child in church. I turn it slowly. It is clearly used, which I like. It unfolds in cascades to the size of a tablecloth. It's not a "veil" to me now, not in the way I used to think of such things. I've seen women only obliquely here in three months, mostly through the effects of their toils. This plain *hijab* is a kind of power, really, like water over rock or like earth that sends first weeds and then grasses up through any crack in the pavement doomed to impermanence. It's an ironic power, a gossamer scantness swathing all the old women in the Gaza Strip where the most apparent power comes all in thicknesses and hardnesses and opacity. Delicacy and gentleness such as this is a kind of defiance here. They who wear this *hijab* tend the children and leaven the bread and hide the food for the curfew; they scoop, sweeten and stir the ten thousand cups of tea that with a hundred thousand other acts of endurance keep the communities up and down the Gaza Strip from annihilation in the siege of canvas and leather and metal, day after day after day.

I refold it carefully and lay it in my bag. I'm alone in the living room. The older kids are at school. Salah is in the bedroom with Mohammed, asleep. I look around. Here is the faded green, mock-velvet chair I sat in on my first night visiting Mohammed last summer, where I sat and watched as men played fast chess and I felt ignorant and small among them. This little round table, its cracked glass top latticed with peeling strips of plastic packaging tape, has held coffee, tea, ashtrays of the cigarettes smoked in conversation, photographs, bowls of fruit, martyr's elegies and whole lunches. The couches, with their overworn cushions and carefully placed white doilies on each armrest, have been full of men who all stood, shook hands, and left them empty, minutes before each night's curfew.

The pictures on the walls are the same as when I arrived. There is the Arab crowd in flight, backs piled high with the remains of households under the black sky and the angry eyes of God that stare out at the viewer. There is the weeping man and the bleeding dove, two unframed paintings. There are the stylized faces of the Arab man and woman, standing with pride and confusion as flames ravage the outline of Palestine over their heads. There is the graduation photo of Mohammed in cap and gown; the tiny embroidered map of Palestine; a prayer from the Qur'an; and, under the bare fluorescent tube that plays surrogate for the light of Heaven, the ceramic relief of the Dome of the Rock. None are exotic anymore. They are understandable products of daily life, spirits from homes, streets, checkpoints and from among the whorls of razor wire at the edge of Canada Camp.

I try to fend off a wave of despair. By now, this feels like a very ordinary Gazan activity, too. When I think of Gaza's future, images of Native American reservations fill my head. Closure only seems to make this image more palpable still, even pragmatic. Mohammed and I talked about this last night. He tended to listen and nod as I explained what happened in my country when the original inhabitants were faced with an expansionism sanctioned by what the newcomers called God. We named it Manifest Destiny, I told him.

Amal—what is the texture of hope as I've seen it in the southern Gaza Strip in this time? The youthful hope drawn in the broad strokes of revolution, the hope of *intifada*, of "shaking off," seems mostly a memory. No one in three months has spoken much of it, although it continues, nominally, inertially, a legacy of a disciplined, unified defiance decaying into splintered, leaderless and increasingly desperate militancy. The diplomatic hope that took wing in Madrid, in October 1991, well, nobody talks about that longer than it takes to scoff at it. Dr. Haidar Abd Al Shafi, chief negotiator and one of the team's only Gazans, is threatening these days to quit the team altogether, pressured as he is by the nearly complete lack of support for the process in his native Gaza Strip. The very words "peace process" bring only scorn here. What's left is the mongrel hope, the survivor's hope, the dull and drubbed and now and then vicious hope. It's the hope of those who know that as long as they still have each other, they will never be entirely vanquished.

Aysha and Suzanne continue to roll the day's bread. I can hear the soft thumping rhythm of their rollers, the patting of their hands and the slap of each loaf on the tray. A helicopter thwacks above, its mission unknowable but always ominous.

Mohammed emerges from the bedroom, finally. He's holding his hand to his forehead, complaining of a headache induced by a rambunctious two-year-old.

"Did you hear shitting at seven o'clock?" he asks me.

"What?! You mean shooting?" I grin.

"Shooting, yes. No—not shitting!" The humor of his mistake earns a brief smile.

"Was it six shots, pa-pa, pa-pa, pa-pa, like that?"

"Yes."

"I heard them," I say. But I had hardly noticed. They weren't followed by ambulance sirens or jeeps. I record this final level of distortion in my sense of what is normal. I gather my bags for the trip, first back to Rimal, tomorrow to Egypt, and then home to the U.S. I work quickly, leaving the rest of the day for farewell visits.

CHAPTER 13
"WE ARE JUST WAITING"

From Gaza city to the Egyptian border terminal there leaves, each morning, the Gaza Strip's only Israeli public bus. Bus 033 heads south from an inconspicuous private taxi station in Rimal at 9:00 except on strike days, curfew days and Fridays.

The driver is Gazan, and so are the eleven other passengers. The license plate, however, is yellow, and the bus is painted the standard Israeli red-orange. Only one window is spiderwebbed from a stone: I find this remarkable considering the fate of the Tel Aviv accountant who drove yellow-plated into Rafah.

We keep to the coast road, the settlers' road around Gaza city, Deir al Balah and Khan Yunis. We crest scrubby dunes, pass scraggly farms with the naked vines of out-of-season grape arbors. At the Gush Qatif settlement bloc, we run the checkpoint—it takes my breath. The soldiers, of course, note the yellow plate, and their expressions don't change as we pass.

Israeli settlements blur by. Prim white, prefab, nuclear-family-sized houses with sloping, tile roofs and paved driveways, suburban subdivisions in the sand, enclosed by high fences, accessible through gates past well-armed guards. Some look inhabited, others not. Some have rows of plastic-covered greenhouses in back; others are simply residential. In one, a synagogue rises, shaped like a giant Star of David. A decade ago the Israeli government was predicting 100,000 settlers would take to the Strip's eighteen settlements, but despite the subsidies and other financial enticements, only 3,500 are here in 1993.

As we near Rafah, I realize something else astonishing for the densely populated Strip: this entire road betrays virtually no evidence that a single Palestinian lives here.

We swing left and traverse the width of the Strip just north of Tel el Sultan and Rafah. At Muraj checkpoint, for the first time I approach without adrenaline. Again the soldiers ignore the bus, and, as we pass, two lines of Peugeots and Mercedes stretch north and south from the checkpoint, waiting.

Our measured immunity ends rudely at the border station. A plainclothes soldier steps on board, his muscles contouring his white T-shirt, cradling his M-16 high so he can sight accurately straight down the barrel at our faces. He pans the gun slowly over each passenger, not saying a word or even gesturing. Everyone reaches—slowly and deliberately—into a pocket, pulls out a Palestinian-only travel document and holds it, unmoving, above his or her head. The soldier appears to use the telescopic sight to read the fine print on every one. Satisfied, he backs down, keeping us in his sights as he does, and still no one has spoken a word. It is the occupation's goodbye. What a contrast to my farewells at Mohammed's and in Tel el Sultan, where the women had prepared *makhluba*, the chicken and rice dish that had become my favorite, and where Mohammed and I had spoken little, because by then no more words had been needed. From outside the bus, the soldier keeps his aim at us through the windows.

Everyone passes through the terminal without so much as an argument. I find this surprising. Stories of Israeli harassment of Palestinians at border crossings—the Allenby bridge to Jordan is the worst, I hear—are legion in the lore of occupation. But I have yet to witness it personally. I find this odd.

By evening I am walking again up unpaved Middle Street to the Khadija Bint Khoweilid elementary, middle and secondary school, the de facto headquarters of Canada Camp, Egypt.

The night is still. The UNRWA ration distribution team has been delayed until tomorrow. Stars glitter through electric wires. From somewhere, the yelp of a boy. From another house, a bang of pots. From the school yard, shouts and the soft thuds of sneakers impacting a soccer ball. Stiff-limbed and

Hairdressing class for young women, Canada Camp Egypt. Very few families can afford to send female children to Egyptian universities. The uncertainty of repatriation has created a complex and difficult marriage environment for both men and women in the camp.

unsmiling, Ahmed the security guard hauls two plastic chairs out onto the sand of the compound and we share tea, a two-man grandstand. He watches without expression. The game ends with the day's final prayer call, which, with no wind, we hear cast from mosques on both sides of the border.

Abu Hassan, UNRWA's camp director, materializes from nowhere, hands in the pockets of his beige overcoat. He is smiling faintly.

"So what's new since two months ago?" I ask.

"Nothing good," he says. UNRWA's $25 million deficit, a result of some UN pledging countries not paying up on time, just forced the layoffs of both of the camp's social workers and three of the seven garbagemen. He says this flatly, saving emotion for more serious matters.

Conversational momentum is low. I try to think of something to say. I know there has been no progress on the funding for Canada Camp family repatriation, so I avoid that right now.

"How are the new classes for women going?" I venture.

"Okay," he says, flopping his hand in the air. "You know some 150 of the young women applied for the ninety-three spots. Sixty-five in sewing, sixteen in hairdressing and twelve in knitting. It helps some, but you know it doesn't really address their situation of being unable to marry." He looks away.

What is a relaxing evening for me is for him and Ahmed just another night of heavy ennui doing time. In a few minutes I accompany Ahmed to a grocery. Our movements are slow, as if each step was the result of a random event.

At the house-front store I tell a couple of men about the photo interviews Mohammed and I did among their former neighbors, the repatriates in Canada Camp Palestine. One flips through a small stack of photos I am carrying. The muscles around his eyes tighten visibly at my shot of Ansar II prison.

"Our future is in Gaza, you know, but this—" he cuts himself off, his head tilted toward the border. His tone suddenly becomes curt. "We are just waiting. That's all I can say. Please do not write anything about politics."

I tell him I don't even know his name, and that he didn't really say anything about politics anyway.

"We have to be so quiet," he replies. "Even when our politics are good ones, favorable ones, we cannot say anything, nothing at all here. Not until we go back."

They leave down the street. Ahmed does not come with me to the school. His shift is over, he says. "You know where to find blankets and mats in the 'Hilton,' right?"

I walk back alone. It's after curfew across the border. This thought brings on a brief giddiness, that of prisoner freed, even in myself. Here life might be dull, and oppressive in its own way, but the questions that dominate Gazan conversations are absent: What happened? How many injured? Any martyrs? Is there curfew? Is there strike tomorrow? How is the road? Are they checking hard at the checkpoint? Did you hear that . . .

The next morning I find Raji, the carpenter. He's sitting on the thin plastic mat in his "porch," the patch of earth in front of his house roofed with chunks of corrugated metal. He doesn't look well. We had parted in February saying, "See you in Palestine, *insha'allah*," for his family is on the list of the next thirty-five due to be repatriated. In February, he was still holding out hope the $12,000 assistance checks might appear from the PLO, God or anyone. Either that or he was in denial that the funding was truly shut off. Now, seven months behind schedule, the reality is starkly apparent. He hasn't shaved for several days. He may have slept in the same red drawstring jogging pants he has on now. His ill-stocked shop is open, no customers; his carpentry shop is as dark and as idle as when we first met.

We are joined quickly by several other men. All look ragged to my eyes, even by Gazan camp standards. Their clothes are torn and unwashed. They tell me they are all from this part of Block B, from the next group due for repatriation. Abandonment and falling self-esteem seem palpable in their very appearance.

Raji pours me tea and demands bluntly, "Where are the pictures?"

I try to take his insistence as a sign of friendship rather than rudeness. I pull out the package full of photos I've prepared to give away. He and two others paw through them, voraciously devouring each image with their eyes in a fraction of a second. One picture of him, Raji says, isn't there. "Why not?!" he says, lowering his brow, shaking the stack in his hand.

I try to explain the economic necessity of editing, that I can't afford prints of each of the hundreds of pictures I take, and I have to choose a few for each of several dozen people. "But if there is one you remember I took but you don't see, I can send it from the States."

"I must keep these," he says, gripping a wad of pictures, at least half the stack.

"Raji," I try to explain diplomatically, "I made these for the people in the pictures. If you take them then you have to give them away to each of these people."

"Yes, yes, okay," he says, seeming agitated. "No problem."

"Everyone will ask me for pictures, just as you have, and when they do, I will tell them to come to you, right?"

"Yes, yes."

I guess he is after a fleeting status that might come with this commission to distribute photos, and I must trust he will not hoard them. After all, if he doesn't give them away, he'll face some angry neighbors.

We just sit. Raji isn't much for conversation today. The morning sun pushes sharp shadows opposite its path. As I am shaking hands to leave, they remind me the eleventh anniversary of *el silik*, the wire, the border of their exile, comes up next week, April 25th. The whole mood disturbs me.

At the tiny camp health clinic, Dr. Nazmi Awad is furiously busy, as usual, trying to keep to his necessary average of six minutes per patient. He questions, takes pulses, checks blood pressures, dispenses pills in tiny paper bags, pops a vaccination now and then into an arm, occasionally lights up a cigarette and plows on through the daily caseload, nearly a dozen waiting outside on benches when I arrive. What, I ask in between patients, about the families who were supposed to repatriate to Tel el Sultan last September?

"I don't think they are much different now from anyone else here. Maybe more stress," he says, "a few more things for them than others. It's a psychological matter. The more time goes on here, the harder it becomes for everyone." A woman enters with a teary young girl, and he doesn't have time to elaborate on what his tone says is obvious.

When I return to the school, ration supplies are arriving by the truckload. Fifty-kilo sacks of flour, sugar and rice are hauled on backs and piled in the big shed in the sweaty, weary, bimonthly ritual.

In the classroom known affectionately by the distribution team as "Hilton Canada," it is party time again, Canada Camp style. Blankets cover the floor, shoes are off, a yellow tongue of propane flame wraps a blackened teapot and the air hangs, viscous with smoke. I share a cigarette with Khalil Audeh, the team coordinator and now my host for another visit with the team.

Old Abu Khaled, who I will always remember as the only one bold enough ever to shout "fuck America" to the face of an American guest, spots me, staggers over, squints at me through his absurdly thick glasses, blinking, and begins bellowing, "Halloo! *salaam alaykum*! Welcome!" over and over. I grab his wrinkled hand and shout back so he can hear me, remembering he is also nearly deaf.

He asks about my stay in Canada Camp this time, and I tell him I am leaving in two days for home, back to the United States.

"And your wife will go with you?" he asks.

"No, my wife is there now, at our home. She was never here," I clarify.

"Hooo! Hooo!" he begins raving, rocking back and forth, recklessly swinging his cane, missing our heads by inches. Everyone begins laughing at him again. "Hooo! He is going to America! Hooo! Hooo! He gets to fuck his American wife! Eeeeyaaa!" He drops to his knees consumed in wicked cackling, and the dozen men join in raucous hooting along with him.

His gleeful, uninhibited obscenity—which I am gathering is one of his social trademarks—earns him the floor for the next two hours. We nibble white cheese and bread with cucumbers and share coffee with abandon. Abu Khaled makes up a nonsense song everyone picks up, and every now and then drops in more naughty wisecracks. He is the only Gazan who has ever done anything remotely like this in my presence. He must just be old enough to get away with it. I am fascinated.

"Crazy! Crazy!" he yells. "Only straw in my brain! And donkey down here!" He starts pulling up his *jalabeeya* only to be restrained by what has become his adoring audience. He sucks on another chain-smoked cigarette so hard his cheeks reveal the contours of his remaining teeth.

Khalil leans over to me. "Don't forget him," he says, the first serious words I've heard in an hour. "I mean it, don't."

"How in the world could I?" I reply, grinning.

"Abu Khaled the Magnificent," he says, as if to make sure I don't write him off as a loon. "He is our clown. With him, we have fun. We laugh. When else do we do that here?"

By early morning, the ration distribution is on. The line of men, women and children bearing old sacks, dirty plastic jugs and the red ration tickets snakes about the school yard. I make a few photographs, but mostly I field requests to see the gift picture packet. Those I send to Raji tend to scowl, making me wonder about his real status in the camp. A few men I don't ever recall actually photographing, yet they insist, and they are disappointed. Those who find pictures often complain they are black and white, not color; that they are small, not large; that there is only one or two of each, not more. I tire quickly of explaining the limitations of my position and leaving people with more promises of more pictures sent from the U.S. Upon hearing these promises, more than one comments they've heard journalists make promises before and they never see anything, really. I say I understand and repeat my promise, meaning it, but still feeling hollow, unable to shed the cloak I wear in their eyes of just another liberal photographer about to leave and forget, using the community for career satisfaction. Would it actually have been more fair to do what I did here in 1989, I wonder, just drop in for a day "parachute" style, saying "Sorry, but all this film is going to New York," and "No, I might never come back"? Could that be more honest than this apparently inadequate charade of reciprocity, of relationship?

Amidst these demands, still other men carry on efforts to direct my day's shooting. I am told to photograph this, or that, usually in harsh tones. Sometimes I do, sometimes not. There seems to be a subtle competition for who can get the foreign photographer to follow his directions the most.

After an hour I retreat into the bunkroom, back to my "Hilton." The demands have become overwhelming. I sit and recall a comment from a psychologist friend of Mohammed's I'd met briefly one night after my visit to Canada Camp Egypt in February. I burrow through my pack to my notebooks, looking for what he'd said.

"We are a society with no stimulation," I had recorded. "It is worse in Canada Camp. Here in the Gaza Strip, at least we can see soldiers, project and ventilate our anger against them. But in Canada Camp they cannot do this. Thus their stress is really above the level of ours. And when a foreigner arrives, it is like something special. Just someone new, someone who looks different, who looks healthy. There is a fascination all out of proportion to the actual event just because there is no other stimulation." Under stress, he had continued, people, in general, become demanding.

But as a photographer I am involved in a further dynamic out there in the yard of the Khadija Bint Khoweilid school. Photography is a taking and, on the part of the photographed, a giving. As critics have long noted, every photographic act involves a negotiation of power, either implicitly or explicitly. Here it could not be more explicit. The men who tug my sleeves to direct my shooting, the ones who insist on prints of every shot I took of them last February, who insist even upon taking the negatives so they can get prints for all their relatives, well, I am finding room for admiration behind my frustration. Their assertions may be the only way, given their situation, to hold on to something of their power, to not submit uncritically to my outsider's decisions and presumption of ownership of pictures. There is a rebellion going on out there, directing my shooting to fit what they want made for their personal use. It's both shield and frontal assault, this refusal of passivity in front of the lens. That the old hierarchy of photographer and "subject"—this latter in every sense of the word—is exactly what Mohammed and I tried so hard to break down by our photo-interview sessions in Canada Camp Palestine. We sure can't do that here, not in Canada Camp Egypt, not under the eyes of the Egyptian intelligence that keeps everyone afraid of speaking honestly with outsiders, afraid such talk might compromise their ability to go home one day.

I walk out of the school feeling frustrated and uncertain of direction. From the top of the street I spot far off, across the border, a half dozen tiny figures, dark lumps of sun and shadow through the layered tangle of *el silik*. They look as though they are waiting for someone. I amble cautiously toward The Calling Wall, alert for Egyptian soldiers as I'm still under official prohibition to go there. None spot me. I lay my hands on the wall's cool, abrasive, unpainted cinder blocks. The wall is shoulder high and sloppily mortared, maybe fifteen feet long. The dirt below me is smooth, packed by feet. I find if I keep my back to another, higher wall of the Egyptian border guardhouse where it meets The Calling Wall, that with my head ducked just below the cinder blocks, the Egyptian soldiers can't see me as they patrol in front, alert to what each person shouts. I wait.

A light-skinned young man with sandy hair, wearing a wrinkled white *jalabeeya*, drives up in a Chevy pickup. He sets the brake and in the same motion jumps out and jogs the few steps to a loose cinder block at the foot of the wall. From it he gains six inches to gaze better at what he briefly tells me is his sister's family. Some boys just fetched him from his house. He adds his sister and her two children can afford to visit Canada Camp Egypt only every other year. He can't afford to visit over there at all. He yells to them.

"How are you!"

"Thanks be to God!" comes the reply.

"How is our father!"

"Thanks be to God!"

He asks how each member of the family is doing, one by one, and receives virtually the same reply, "Thanks be to

God," embellished with a few details, for each one. It takes a long time, and the news, being spoken so publicly, is superficial, even banal. The purpose of the visit seems to be just to see each other, to stand, despite the soldiers and the wires and the thirty-yard gulf, in each other's affirming presence. It takes effort to come here. The making of this effort is thus perhaps the most important communication of all.

Two women approach the wall now, looking like mother and daughter. They begin calling to a second family that has appeared in a small huddle on the other side. The women stand between me and the sandy-haired man. The Calling Wall is like a party line, and their shouts quickly drown out those of the man next to them.

"How are you!" the young woman near me shouts.

"Fine, fine, thanks be to God! How are all of you!"

"Okay, thanks to God. Why didn't you come last week? Where have you been?" She turns her head each time she finishes, directing her left ear to Palestine, her eyebrows tense in concentration. She faces me without meeting my eyes. Her mother stands to her left, waving her hand aloft.

"It was curfew here!" they shout back.

"How's Zeina!" she yells.

"Fine!" A man on the other side hoists up a small girl in a red dress and dangles her over the razor wire like a large floppy doll. She waves. The women echo the girl with big, sweeping, slow-motion waves, the kind to be seen from far away. Fifteen years from now, will Zeina say, "Yes, I remember my aunts, I would wave to them as my father held me by my waist over the sharp wires, and then I would ask, 'why can't we visit them?'"

The woman next to me is all in black. She rises slightly now on tiptoe in her pointed, mirror-polished shoes, propping her arms and shoulders on top of the blocks, leaning forward to shave a few inches off the despicable distance, clenching a fist near her mouth. Her eyes are damp. She dabs at them, once each, with her black sleeve, careful not to smear mascara. Her mother does the shouting now.

Another old woman approaches the wall. "Is anyone talking to anyone from Shaboura?" she asks.

"Yes, *haji*," says the man with the sandy hair, using the polite form of address to a woman beyond childbearing years. "My sister is from Shaboura. What do you want?"

"I have a message for my son. I want him to meet me here at four o'clock tomorrow, *insha'allah*. His name is Mustafa Aziz, Abu Jihad."

The man turns back toward his family and calls to them, "Do you know Mustafa Aziz!"

"Who?!"

"Mustafa Aziz! Abu Jihad! From Shaboura!"

"No!"

"Find someone who knows him and tell him to come tomorrow at four o'clock, *insha'allah*."

"Mustafa Aziz Abu Jihad?! Four o'clock?"

"Yes!"

"Insha'allah!"

After a few minutes, the man says goodbye to his family, waves, and heads back to his pickup. The two women follow shortly, not speaking as they slip back into Canada Camp.

I'm left alone in my hidden corner. The sun burns now out of the sky flat with haze. The talk of the Egyptian soldiers filters over, languid and unintelligible. Two Israeli guards sit motionless in the high window of their guardhouse. I wait for others to come to call to someone, but no one does. I rest my chin on my hands on top of the wall and stare over into Rafah, Gaza Strip, occupied Palestine, Rafah derided and despised by nearly everyone, yet the very place of dreams and deepest longing for all those who next week will pass into their twelfth year in this sad and listless camp. Rafah tumbles its monochrome concrete at me through the sinuous barbed wire, razor wire, chain-link wire. A few almond trees. A few cactus. Smoke from somewhere, perhaps a tire set aflame by *shabab*. Far away, a young girl walks alone. On border patrol, on the road between fences, an Israeli army jeep hums from afar and blurs by, smearing brown dust across Rafah's colorless sky.

I am the child of Palestine
I have my cause and I have my rights
When I see my older brother
Taken up into outlaws' hands
I cry out the international cry
That if they shoot me to my death
I'll clutch a stone in my right hand
And never forget the martyrs' cause.
    —*translated nursery rhyme, as sung by a five-*
        year-old girl, Khan Yunis, March 1994

EPILOGUE

A year later, in March 1994, I returned to see how people were responding to the Israeli-PLO accord of September 1993. Over a month's visit, I was reminded that while events inevitably outpace those who try to write about them, the changes that follow upon events are shadows of a far slower, far more complex and uncertain process. I was also reminded of the extent to which words that permeate Western discussion of Israeli-Palestinian affairs— *redeployment, autonomy, peace, development, democracy* and, of course, *occupation*, to name a few—carry entirely different meanings inside the Gaza Strip.

This time I can visit Canada Camp Egypt only for a few hours. It is Ramadan again, and less than two weeks following what is now simply "the massacre," meaning the February 25, 1994, killing of Palestinian worshippers at Hebron's Ibrahimi Mosque.

During the scratchy phone calls from the U.S. I had been warned it might not be possible to visit at all. I try to feel some gratitude for that rather than anger at the camp's enduring, forcible isolation, but I can't convince myself. Months ago, in October, when the government of Canada announced its revival of the camp's repatriation assistance account, I had hoped that this visit might at last be the one on which I would photograph the joyful scenes of families going home. But the funds are in limbo awaiting approval from an Israeli government preoccupied with more pressing matters of the Gaza Strip's nominal transition to PLO authority. Thus, it is into a mostly unchanged atmosphere of blank waiting that I ride the shared taxi from Cairo across Sinai's sands, an atmosphere that has become more of Canada Camp's story than repatriation can ever be now.

"You know I like to be hospitable, Dick. It is such a pleasure to receive a visitor, it breaks the boredom," says Abu Hassan when I arrive. His camp director's office in the Khadija Bint Khoweilid school is, as always, a tidy island of dignity. "But with the people so angry after the massacre, we are under heavier eyes than at any time I can remember. So I am afraid we can only talk inside this office for a few hours and then you must leave. And no photographs. I'm sorry. I wish I could welcome you to *iftar* at my house." His face hangs in a way I haven't seen before.

He excuses himself and lifts a white phone. He brightens his voice to announce my name, passport number and purpose of visit to the officer at Egyptian State Security Investigation, the *mukhabarat*. When he hangs up, his mood darkens again like flipping out the lights.

"I must do this. You must understand. If I do not, they can make many, many problems. They will know you have come."

I nod. I had to come alone. The date of the next UNRWA rations distribution is uncertain due to the upcoming change of authority in the Gaza Strip. Abu Hassan helps me with a list of questions and assures me he will distribute the stack of photographs I had hoped to pass out in the camp myself. His expression stays wooden.

"In my heart and soul, I feel like I am dead," he tells me later in a quiet voice without meeting my eyes. "When I eat, I don't feel I can even taste it. Every day here is like taking a step, but you put your foot in the same footprint of yesterday. There is no progress. So we have depression. Every family here would go over tomorrow, without money, without anything, if only Israel would permit us. But they say we must have [the repatriation assistance] money. So. Maybe some families go this year, maybe not. Thirty-five families each year, only. It will take ten years, at least. Ten years!" He looks up at me, shrugs, and turns away.

In Khan Yunis, my first glimpse of the rooftop flags, illegal until last September 13, brings a wave of an unfamiliar emotion, something between relief at this tangible sign of political achievement and sadness that the constant gray around the flags makes them look so small. Mohammed will not be at home. He is in England studying for his master's degree. I visited him on my way from the United States, and thus I walk the street to his house bearing his letters, photos and promises of proxy hugs to children. I step over the dribble of sewage in front of the sagging house, under a line of laundry, and through the back door.

Reunion explodes the routine of the family afternoon. One, two, three, soon eight kids are shrieking as I lift each for a hug; I kiss the cheeks of Mohammed's brothers four, six times and shake hands with all the women once, twice. As the hellos and welcomes and inquiries about well-being dance among us, again I am reminded of what has held Gazan society together through occupation: families. Beaming, Khaled nearly drops a blanket-wrapped infant into my arms. Feiras, he names the child, born to Suzanne and him in December. I count months out loud since their wedding the day the Israeli army demolished homes in *amal mashroua*, Hope Project, and kid him about their speed. This is a compliment, and his grin widens.

After tea, I hand Ibtisam, Mohammed's wife, an envelope of photographs: Mohammed wearing a tie and English tweeds; Mohammed tapping at computer terminals; Mohammed cooking with friends in his dormitory she will never see. It's been five months since he left. The joy of my arrival dissipates quickly because I arrived without him. Here in this house, as a male visitor, I still do not know how to ask her honestly, as a woman, about her stress of being alone with three children in occupied Khan Yunis. I just ask how she is doing; she says "Thanks be to God," and lets only the resignation in her voice slip over the barrier between us.

Rateb, Mohammed's elder brother, tells me he found work

last fall designing chicken-feed processing machinery in the central Strip. The job pays one-fourth of what he used to make in Israel. *"Ahsan min balash"*—"better than nothing," he says, "there are too many now who have only nothing." After *iftar* as we relax on mats with tea in the television room, he tells me how he had to give up on searching for work in Israel soon after I left last year. The permanent closure of the Strip and West Bank that began March 29 was partially relaxed over the summer. By fall, just more than half the workers had returned. But without a preexisting job, Rateb couldn't be among those to receive the permission slips. Inside the Strip, closure had been an economic disaster. Unable to import key materials, what little industry is permitted inside the Strip dried up while consequent unemployment further flooded the labor market. The average daily wage plunged two dollars' equivalent. Unemployment is still above 50 percent, and most of the "employed" are in fact working only part-time.

Today, Rateb says, he lost another day's wages. The army mounted the thirty-second artillery attack on family homes since the June 1992 inauguration of Prime Minister Rabin, and the third attack since the September Israel-PLO accord. Seven homes were felled near Rateb's worksite; the army claims it suspected activists were inside; the area was under curfew today.

The next afternoon, Ahmed drops by, lanky, now twenty-four, grinning but looking worn. His black hair is cut neatly for the *eid al fitr* celebration, the end of Ramadan, coming up in three days. We grew close last year. Since I left, his scholarship to Sudan never came through, and worse, he'd spent part of the year in prison. I had worried about him, and our reunion is heartfelt.

Together we negotiate a path downtown, avoiding omnipresent, sloppy puddles of muck.

"So what's different in Khan Yunis since last year?" I ask.

Ahmed points out the black flags peppering the sky along with the national colors from housetops. "Those are for the massacre," he says. "They mean people want revenge. You know the massacre was not only in Hebron."

I nod. After the news of the massacre broke, five Gazans had been killed and more than 370 injured when the army crushed street marches. Still others died in protests in the West Bank. "Now look at people's faces," he instructs me. "And see how they move in the street. Watch. See how they are walking. You will see the difference."

"It looks the same to me."

"No. It isn't. See that man? He is walking slowly, his head is down. He is bored, depressed. There is no life in the way he walks. Many people are now like this, no job, no money. We are three days before the feast day. Israel is closed again since two weeks, since the massacre. He will not be able to buy any one thing for his children." He takes me by the arm to the market and shows me a narrow street full of second-hand clothes merchants. "For the feast," he says. "Not so many of us buying new clothes as is our custom. Just this."

I watch a small crowd surround a man auctioning off used dresses, skirts, shirts and jeans from the back of a truck. Yesterday, Rowhi, Mohammed's former boss from the Rafah Social Welfare Office, had told me that since the closure last March excess applications for limited UNRWA rations have shot from 2,000 to above 15,000 in Rafah alone. "We are turning away hundreds and hundreds of otherwise eligible families," he said. Similarly, the vice-chairman of Gaza's Islamic charitable society, Yusef Za'im, told me before I arrived in Khan Yunis that his biggest problem now was a burgeoning "hidden poor." These, he explained, are families who until this year were the charity's donors. "Merchants with popular shops, employees in Israel, landowners—these people will not come to us for help even if they starve to death! We must go about the city in the evening asking who knows who might need some rice, some flour. We then give it quietly, in the back door. You would not believe how many people are hungry, and out of pride they will never admit it to anyone, not to UNRWA, not to you or even to us."

Ahmed and I walk back into the camp, the west end of town. In the late afternoon light we watch masked youths bearing knives, hatchets and one with a pistol run more freely than I saw last year, spray-painting graffiti and wheat-pasting posters to walls. He confirms for me the black-market prices for the guns I'd read had become so common: $10,000 for an M-16; $7,000 for a *klashin*, or Kalashnikov AK-47; $8,000 for an Uzi; and $3,000–$4,000 for a pistol. Family savings, he says, are being squandered out of fear of factional warfare and the desire by some to revive the armed threat to Israel.

This is borne out by statistics. Since the accord, the Strip has become a more violent place than at any time since the beginning of the *intifada* in 1987 and 1988. Palestinian attacks against Israeli soldiers and settlers inside the Strip, and less-frequent attacks on Israeli civilians inside Israel, have risen to an average of forty-two a month since September, eight to ten times the rate they occurred last year, according to UNRWA. The Israeli army, however, against the background of promises of imminent redeployment, has killed 105 Gazans and injured an appalling 6,673 since I left last April, according to the Gaza Center for Rights and Law. The injured in this period alone are nearly one percent of the population of the Gaza Strip.

"There is no peace treaty here," Ahmed says as we arrive at his house at the edge of the camp. He points to a new Israeli watchtower, sandbagged and sporting an Israeli flag, from the half-shuttered window of his tiny concrete living room. "That will be the new border, they say. They say they will withdraw, but to where? To there? That is not withdrawal, that is a settlement, it is our land! They will come into the camp when they want and shoot. Under the agreement, our police will have no authority over them. What kind of police is that? None of their laws will change."

"And Arafat?" I ask. "What do you think of him now?"

"Still the majority of the families here, especially the oldest and most powerful ones, all support the PLO and Arafat. It is still in their interest, economically and politically. They will gain from this agreement. But for us, for the refugees? He sold out the *intifada*."

Like Khan Yunis, Canada Camp Palestine appears little changed. A group of boys guides me about at first, pointing out the new soccer field, the two new speakers wired to the mosque so people in Canada Camp Palestine now hear prayer calls better, and the pair of ping-pong tables purchased by one of Abu Yasser's sons and now set up in the family garage and open to the public. A few families, they say, added floors to their cinder-block homes. But still the dumpsters overflow, still the streets are all sand, and still there is not a telephone to be found. Three boys are serving six-month terms in Ketziot prison after soldiers picked them up and accused them of stone-throwing.

At the house of Hanan, head teacher of Rafah Girls' School "D," I find her clothed in black. It is the first time I've seen her without color at least in her *hijab*. But before I can say anything, and almost before I can finish what I consider a proper greeting, she holds her hand up to interrupt me. Yesterday, she announces, she fixed the marriage of her oldest daughter to an engineer, "a very, very good young man." She smiles proudly, awaiting my reaction. I shower her with the customary, effusive congratulations, and she motions me to the brown velour couch under the un-refugee-like glass chandelier.

She calls to her husband and daughters, and the family gathers hastily. With the wedding upcoming, she apologizes, this may be our only chance to talk. We don't tarry on family matters this time; I ask what the September peace accord means to them.

"The agreement was like a dream at first," says Nisreen, twenty-four, who was at school in Egypt last year. "We celebrated at first, of course. It was like a woman who for forty-five years has tried to become pregnant, and finally she succeeds. But now the child has died before being born, or if it is born, it will be a cripple."

"In the beginning of the agreement we thought maybe there was hope," echoes Hanan. The pleasure of the wedding announcement has left her. "Now, some days I feel like I have fallen down a well." She shakes her head slowly.

"Here in Rafah it is the worst," she continues, explaining that it is because Rafah has the most refugees, the deepest poverty and "it is we, the refugees, who have lost the most now. The agreement means we will not ever go back to our land, and we will not ever receive any kind of compensation for what was stolen. Abu Ammar [Yasser Arafat] signed this hope away."

"But I thought three-fourths of people here supported the agreement, at least in September. Everyone danced in the streets. What happened?" I ask.

They piece together a litany of confidence-breaking events on both sides. Arafat's Fateh acted autocratically by signing an agreement without the consent of the people in the first place, I hear. The accord, they continue, implicitly recognized the legality of Israeli settlements, which they took as tantamount to Arafat's stamp of approval on land theft. Israel has continued relentlessly in house-to-house searches and home demolitions. In December, Israel betrayed Ahmed Abu Reesh, a Fateh militant, by granting him amnesty and then deploying an Israeli undercover unit to assassinate him outside his home, in front of friends and relatives, a week later. Israel has failed to release nearly 10,000 political prisoners as promised; failed to meet the December 13, 1993, withdrawal deadline as promised; and, now, has responded to the massacre in Hebron not with compensatory confidence-building, but with stepped-up economic and military repression.

We sit in silence for a moment. Their desolation is disorienting to me. I am feeling desperate to hear hope. Surely the half-full glass, though spilt, cannot yet be entirely empty.

"Won't it help," I say, "to get the army out and economic aid coming in? I mean, they will leave soon, won't they?"

"Israel will limit and define the economy, like always," says Nisreen. "It will be done to make us forget the *intifada*, to make us work only for money, to make us forget all those who died for us. Occupation is not just soldiers in streets."

"What kind of agreement would you still support?"

The family consults and agrees on several points: all prisoners must be released; the Jewish settlements must be removed; separated family members must be allowed re-entry to the Strip; the army must keep to withdrawal deadlines and transfer power according to the terms of the Oslo accord; and, finally, the Israeli military law that will remain in place under the accord must be replaced by law enacted by a democratically elected, Palestinian body. "If this happens," says Nisreen, "there will be a small peace, a kind of peace."

I find Mustafa not at his home in Canada Camp Palestine, but at the sun-drenched villa office of the Save the Children Federation, a U.S.-based aid group, in Gaza's wealthy Rimal district. Amidst the social wreckage of 50 percent unemployment, he has been one of relatively few to benefit, so far, from the 1993 Israel-PLO accord.

Here, his name is on a door with his title, Environmental Projects Coordinator. A shelf inside displays ten varieties of Israeli-made plastic sewer pipes. Desks are littered with proposals, memos and half-drafted budgets. His face is fuller than when he was working construction in Israel last year, and his clothes are new. Window light gleams in his eyes bright now with a sense of purpose.

In May 1993, when he was unable to enter Israel due to closure, he applied for three jobs inside the Strip using his civil engineering degree. With international development money beginning to trickle in, he was offered all three of them. Now, his salary of $900 a month doubles his former wage in Israel, and it comes with family health insurance and use of a car. He directs sewage pipe installation, trash removal and parkland establishment projects up and down the Strip. In his spare time, he will oversee the construction of the Palestinian-Canadian Friendship Community Center in Tel el Sultan, which, he tells me, has just received $125,000 initial funding from the Canadian International Development Agency.

"It will be a center for orientation when the people at last come from Canada Egypt," he says. "We will have kindergarten, daycare, women's classes and youth programs, *insha'allah*." He speaks now as much with his hands as with his voice. "You would not believe how much money is going to come here! Europe, America, Japan, everywhere they want to give us money! Two and a quarter billion dollars! But we must get it soon because people are now so poor and expecting so much change."

I tell him about my conversation with Hanan.

"Hanan, yes," he says, slowing down. "She is viewing the situation from the heart of Rafah, the heart of Canada Camp Palestine. This is like the majority of people. I am seeing it from here, from Gaza and Rimal, where we see visitors and money every day. I believe Israel must allow us to succeed or they face a time bomb. It is in their interest, and they know this."

But "uncertainty" is his answer when, later, I ask him to elaborate his opinion on Gazan zeitgeist. "Every day now, we do not know what will happen to us. We, the people, are not making the decisions for ourselves. Will Israel really leave? How much will they leave? If they do, who—really—will replace them? Will we have freedom or will we be occupied by our own people? You cannot believe how sick I am of this. Every day these questions. And I have a good job! What about those who don't?"

That evening, he invites me to a meeting in Tel el Sultan of the community center committee. He asks me to leave my camera behind, as there will be men there I have never met. Mustafa chairs the gathering of eight. Little cakes and tea make rounds. I sit quietly, and the men discuss funding and construction. As I listen, a small exhilaration rises in me. I remember photographing Mustafa once last year in a far different circle, one of despondent men arranging day labor in Israel. Tonight, at last, I see change and hope: Mustafa is no longer building someone else's country. He is building his own.

I study faces in the dim fluorescent light. In the coming years, history may mark not confrontations and martyrs' funerals as milestones so much as plain-folks meetings like this. Dull to my photojournalist's eyes, tonight's gathering is nevertheless integral to the founding of any country Mustafa, Hanan, Mohammed and all Palestinians might one day have. Through the years of military occupation, here and in the West Bank, people maintained networks and met in countless underground committees. The significance of this is routinely underrated, even neglected, by outsiders whose gaze becomes easy captive to visually compelling poverty and violence. I think about my own former compulsion to photograph confrontations between soldiers and *shabab*. Why did I not have a parallel compulsion to photograph meetings?

Afterwards, as we all walk back toward Mustafa's house, Mustafa is arguing with one of the men.

"I will not let this be politicized!" Mustafa shouts into the nearly-curfew night. "This community center must serve each household and all of the children, not just Fateh, not just Hamas!"

"If he is on the committee we will get nothing done with the authorities," retorts the man, meaning, this time, the PLO authorities. "Maybe not everyone has to be Fateh, but we cannot have one from that group."

Their fight is over a popular community leader who is also the lone Hamas supporter in their group. Partisan conflict over institutional control has intensified over the past year in the Strip. In an article published in June 1993, in the *Journal of Palestine Studies*, author Sara Roy observed that "The creation of *structures*, once a prominent feature of the uprising, is steadily giving way to the creation of *constituencies* in institutional guise."[1] As Mustafa and the man argue, I recall the rainy February day in Rafah when I shook the meaty hand of a civil servant shot in the leg by militants who sought to force the diversification of the Fateh-dominated municipality. Mustafa and the man part without the customary farewell niceties, leaving the dispute unresolved.

It seems that inside the Gaza Strip, there is always something going on behind the headlines. On September 13, 1993, in Washington, D.C., Prime Minister Rabin and Chairman Arafat shook "the handshake heard around the world," while in Gaza city, the Gaza Community Mental Health Center quietly opened its first international conference. What it signified may in the long run mean as much to Gazans as Israeli-PLO rapprochement. The Center's director, psychiatrist Dr. Eyad Al Sarraj, appeared at the podium as a man aged, like so many Gazans, beyond his years.

Although all Palestinians stand in debt to the "children of the stone" who resisted occupation with the *intifada*, Sarraj reflected, it is time to understand fully that "the children of the stone are not made of stone." Drawing from this one simple phrase, Sarraj has laid out a framework for healing in the Gazan future. In 1993, results of the first formal psychological studies in the Gaza Strip forecast it will take at least two generations to begin to heal occupation's abuse. "The extent of [children's] exposure to traumatic events is horrific," he said. "What will become of you, children of the stone? What kind of students are you? What kind of parents will you be, happy and loving or neurotic and abusive? What teachers will we have, what lawyers, what leaders?"

In the audience was Dr. Mahfuz 'Uthman, a British-trained psychologist and a friend of Mohammed's. It was Sarraj, he tells me when I visit him in his Rafah home, who in 1990 began to explore how post-traumatic stress disorder (PTSD) affects Gazans. "It was amazing no one thought of it before he did," he says. "But here among ourselves we have a special problem in the definition of trauma, because after twenty-seven years there is of course enormous habituation to our stress. We don't know what is normal. In our isolation, we have lost sight of any standard. There was an American psychologist at the conference who said because of our continuous trauma, we even have our own variety of PTSD. 'The Gaza Syndrome,' he called it.

And we all suffer from it, even me, of course. For example, one common sign is the difficulty in concentrating because of intrusive thoughts and worries. I was in a gathering of teachers just a few days ago, and I noticed none of us talked about anything for more than a few seconds. These are teachers, I thought, people who are supposed to be thoughtful, intellectual leaders. I realized then this is true all over Gaza, waking and sleeping. We are truly preoccupied by the occupation. The liberation of our own minds may prove to be the most difficult liberation of all."

March 1995

In the weeks before this book goes to press, I call Mohammed. He returned home in September 1994, master's degree in hand, and walked into a Gaza Strip with no nightly curfew and no Israeli soldiers searching homes, a Gaza Strip at the threshold of an ill-defined "autonomy" and still faintly pulsing with September 1993's hope. But the virtual collapse of the "peace process" in early 1995 has made it clear that the cycle of abuse born of occupation has yet to change fundamentally. Most of last year's questions stand unanswered, and the urgency of many has only intensified.

When my call comes in, Mohammed is arriving at UNRWA's Gaza headquarters. He is a community development officer now. It is a good job. After talk of families, he shifts to *el wadd'a.*

"Sometimes I feel like I am crippled anymore in my ability to analyze it all, Dick. I am just trying to live it day to day, which takes all of my energy. We are still cut off [from travel or work in Israel] by the closure, you know. And also, we have now one of the main problems with underdevelopment: Who will teach the teachers?"

"How different is it just to have the army out of the streets?" I ask.

"You know, the feeling is not so different as you might

expect. It is like now, the economic situation has taken over. How do you feel when you go to the market and you have the same money but the price of even the smallest items is double? In Tel el Sultan, the seventy families who came back last summer cannot build more because the price of construction materials has tripled!"

His tone sounds far from his trademark good spirits.

"Some roads are being renovated now, but not in any proper way. There is little electricity. There is no mail. There is no plan! After six months, the power is being concentrated into a few hands. In the *intifada*, everyone volunteered to do this or that with such hope. Now it is not the same motivation at all. Expectations were raised high, and what we see is the opposite."

"You sound demoralized," I say, wanting him to talk more.

"Yes, people are so much demoralized. In Gaza we need years to be educated, to learn about police, about rules and laws and how to have a society that works for all the people."

As I listen I find myself in the sharp, familiar Gazan struggle to keep from losing a thread of hope. So often it had been Mohammed who helped me to find it. Now, for a moment, it seems I must help him. He says each time I call or fax now, it helps him ward off the deepening chill of isolation and uncertainty.

By the time we hang up, I am reminded that the hope in Gaza has changed little, too. It is as ever something we create in the spaces between us. Every act that affirms relatedness breathes life into it and thus, it is not something we merely have, it is something we do.

Note

1. Sara Roy, "Gaza: New Dynamics of Civic Disintegration," *Journal of Palestine Studies*, 12, no. 4 (Summer 1993), 20–31 (italics in original).

The intifada, *December 1987 to May 1994:*
523 Gazans killed by Israeli security forces;
462 Gazan homes demolished by Israeli security forces;
78,388 hospital-registered injuries from Israeli security forces.
Source: The Gaza Center for Rights and Law, affiliate of the
International Commission of Jurists, Geneva

ACKNOWLEDGMENTS

Thanks to the loving support and constant encouragement of Kathryn Kinson, this book exists. Even as she tolerated my absences from home and worked to pay bills during writing, it was her willingness to read and discuss the book on an almost daily basis that led to much of what is good in these pages and excised much of what was not.

Likewise, Trish Reynolds of Kumarian Press was essential in her patience and her firm belief the book was possible. Earlier, in Cairo, Ann Marie Harrison of *Cairo Today* (now *Egypt Today*) generously gave me the time amidst assignment duties to visit Canada Camp.

In Gaza, the hospitality of too many who prefer not to be named stands beyond mere thanking. They include not only interviewees quoted and unquoted, but taxi drivers, women whose cooking sustained me, and strangers whose moments of spontaneous kindness kept me safe. Mohammed and I both thank especially the brave, kind person who first welcomed us into Canada Camp Palestine, as well as Mohammed Al Najjar, Rowhi Ghanam, Khalil Audeh, Khalil Abu Shammallah, Awad El Hawaldeh and Mustafa El Hawi for hospitality, friendship, and favors too many to name. Also in Gaza, Loren Lybarger, Douglas Ierley, Ron Wilkinson, Rolf Van Uye, Rula Halawani, Mark Taylor, Raji Sourani and the Gaza Center for Rights and Law, and Synabel Press were all more than generous at every turn. My greatest personal thanks, however, goes to each member of Mohammed's family, who together taught me a further dimension of love.

To all those who so insightfully reviewed drafts because they cared about what Mohammed and I were doing, thank you: Ibtisam Barakat, Lorraine Chittock, Anelia Dimitrova, my parents Nadine and Bill Doughty, Mae Ghalwash, Mary Grigsby, Steve and Lail Herman, Ann Lesch, Tom Neu, Jack Shaheen and, many times over, Kathryn Kinson. Thanks also to Hugi Neuburg, for the extra help and, as always, the inspiration.

196   GAZA: LEGACY OF OCCUPATION

All this would have been impossible without financial support: The University of Missouri School of Journalism's Duffy Fund and the O. O. McIntyre Postgraduate Writing Fellowship funded fieldwork and initial writing. The Morris journalism internship program of the National Council on U.S.-Arab Relations first took me to the Middle East. The International Summer Program at Birzeit University provided the context in which the problems of living as a foreigner in occupied Gaza could be solved.

INDEX